PREFACE

The New American Schools Development Corporation (NASDC), a private nonprofit corporation, was created in 1991 as part of the America 2000 initiative to fund the development of new, whole-school designs for American schools. NASDC funded teams to develop and demonstrate whole-school designs to increase student performance. This effort was completed in June 1995.

NASDC asked RAND to carry out a formative evaluation of its efforts at whole-school transformation. That evaluation compared and contrasted nine designs and their demonstration strategies and described the sites that became partners with the teams.[1] The descriptions represent a baseline for the design team efforts to help schools move toward self-improvement.

The conceptual framework developed in the baseline document was subsequently used to track the progress of the teams and sites toward the implementation of their designs and the factors that facilitated or impeded that progress. This report analyzes those factors and discusses how the teams have evolved strategies for assisting schools. The report provides lessons learned to more effectively produce whole-school transformations for jurisdictions and schools interested in school improvement.

This report and subsequent ones on the NASDC experience should interest educational policymakers at all levels of government, school

---

[1]Bodilly et al. (1995).

D1367894

administrators and teachers, and communities concerned with improved schooling.

The research was supported by NASDC. The study was conducted under the auspices of RAND's Institute on Education and Training.

LESSONS FROM NEW AMERICAN SCHOOLS DEVELOPMENT

PHASE

Susan Bodilly

with
Susanna Purnell
Kimberly Ramsey
Sarah J. Keith

Institute on Education and Training

Supported by the
New American Schools Development Corporation

RAND

CONTENTS

FIGURES

The New American Schools Development Corporation (NASDC) was established in 1991 to fund the development of organizations that would create designs for "break-the-mold" schools and help schools implement those designs. The notion of NASDC is somewhat unique—to deliberately develop expert organizations that can help schools transform themselves. NASDC's focus has always been on whole-school design, not design of specific subcomponents of schooling; all the designs require a full transformation of the school. If its potential is met, the idea of an expert organization providing both a whole-school design and implementation assistance offers some hope of altering the pattern of failed reform common in schools today. Those pursuing public education reform are interested in the experiences of the NASDC enterprise and whether it encourages permanent improvement in schools.

A national competition by NASDC led to the choice of 11 teams. The teams were given one year, from mid-year 1992 to mid-year 1993 (Phase 1), to build their teams and further develop the concepts of their designs from the visions described in their proposals. In Phase 2, the teams had two years, ending in June 1995, to further develop and to demonstrate and test their designs in real schools. NASDC expected that at the end of two years each team would have a fully developed design, would have tested and demonstrated all elements of the design in at least two sites, and would be fully capable of moving into more schools. Given the results of the demonstrations at the end of Phase 2, NASDC further reduced the number of teams to seven. In Phase 3, now beginning, the seven teams are expected to enter a new group of schools in selected jurisdictions and provide more adept assistance to schools based upon lessons learned and materials developed in Phase 2.

PURPOSE

NASDC asked RAND to perform a formative assessment of the Phase 2 experience to provide the interested public with some indication of the progress made during Phase 2. This report provides that assessment and draws lessons from NASDC's Phase 2 that might be usefully applied to Phase 3 and to school reform efforts in general. Although the demonstration nature of Phase 2 limits the types of lessons that might be learned, in fact the teams and associated sites offer a rich source of information about reform. The report addresses several questions and is organized into chapters that respond to each question:

- What were the essential characteristics and differences among the designs and teams at the beginning of Phase 2?

- How did these characteristics and differences affect progress toward NASDC Phase 2 goals?

- Did the teams develop effective implementation and assistance strategies for whole-school transformation in line with NASDC goals for Phase 2?

- Were there important institutional, cultural, or systemic barriers to reform that need to be addressed to improve the effort?

- Given the answers to the above questions, what has been the collective contribution of NASDC to reform so far?

METHOD

The research uses a comparative case study approach with the design team as the unit of analysis and the nine designs compared and contrasted. Two sites were chosen for each team to form an embedded case study that includes the team, the district, the schools, and individuals associated with the schools. The research team reviewed proposals, design documents, and reports submitted to NASDC by the design teams. In fall 1993, spring 1994, and spring 1995, teams of two staff members visited each design team and two sites associated with each design. District officials, school principals, key design-related site personnel, teachers, parents, students, and business partners were interviewed. The RAND team also conducted informal observations of the schools.

Progress of design teams and sites toward the NASDC goal of full demonstration was tracked across the "elements" of each design. These elements of design were developed by a content analysis of the proposals and are simply categories of change that design teams envisioned, including curriculum and instruction, standards, assessments, student groupings, community involvement, integration of social services, participatory governance within the school, school autonomy from the district, state legislative changes, professional development, and staff and organizational changes at the school. The teams varied as to the changes within an element envisioned and as to the elements covered.

OUTCOMES OF THE FORMATIVE ASSESSMENT OF TEAMS

We found that the teams varied in the progress they made toward the NASDC goal of full demonstration of all elements included in each team's design. The differences in progress were closely associated with several factors: team readiness or capability at the beginning of the NASDC effort, the type of design and approach to development chosen by the team, and the implementation strategy used to infuse the design into schools.

Relative Progress Toward Demonstration Associated with Differences Among Designs and Teams

The readiness of the teams for Phase 2 had a large effect on progress, with several having to develop a staff, stabilize the team leadership, and develop school-based experience in implementation of reform. However, the effect of team readiness on meeting future NASDC goals should lessen in Phase 3 because of the capacity-building accomplished by all teams during Phase 2.

The differences among teams in design and approaches to development had a significant effect on their ability to produce the full demonstration wanted by NASDC within Phase 2. Teams that had developed team capability before the NASDC effort, had fewer design elements, and encouraged significant team responsibility for the specification and development of the design were able to more fully demonstrate the elements of their designs. Newly created teams that included more elements of reform and required significant site-based development of those elements had more work to do to fully demonstrate their designs. Therefore, in the limited time period they did not demonstrate their designs as fully.

The differences in types of designs promise to have continuing effects in Phase 3, with the more comprehensive and systemic designs—those addressing more elements, especially governance, social services, and staffing—taking more time and having greater site-based variation in implementation.

Teams that require sites to develop a significant portion of the design to suit local circumstances (site-based development) will also experience slower and more variable progress toward reform in their associated schools. Site capacity for change proved to be very important for all teams, but especially for those that required significant site-based development. The more elements that required significant site-based development, the more a school's resources were taxed on multiple fronts, implying that schools have an upper limit to the amount of change that can be undertaken and this limit is defined by both available time of teachers and the skills and talents needed to address the design elements.

At the end of Phase 2, the nature of interaction between teams and sites was changing as sites progressed toward the design goals. In reaction to this developmental phenomenon, teams and schools began to focus more on the permanent systemic changes needed to promote and sustain the design in the school without continued intervention by the team. Thus, without necessarily meaning to, all teams arrived at a point where they became concerned with governance changes, improved social services, increased public engagement, and new school staffing and organization.

These findings indicate that there are many pathways to transformed schools. These pathways have real implications for the pace and types of changes that will take place in the schools and must be reflected in expectations that sites have for progress.

A further implication is that much could be done to make schools better consumers for reform. Schools should ask what type of reform is being offered, what level of effort will be required of them, what is the experience of the assistance organization, and whether the school itself has the capability and desire for the particular reform being proposed.

Implementation Strategy

The experiences of Phase 2 reinforce the idea that design and implementation are closely related and both are needed to produce organizational change. Teams developed different strategies for implementation—getting assistance to sites to meet the team's vision of reform. Effective implementation strategies keyed to the design were important in bringing about changes in schools.

Site selection processes did not always produce the commitment necessary to move sites forward quickly. Important elements of a selection strategy included an introduction by the team itself and a vote by all staff. Equally important was a good match between the tenets of the design and the conditions at the school. For example, magnet high schools were not a good match for designs requiring detracking, and high schools priding themselves on their electives were not a good match for designs that called for concentration on a core curriculum.

Initial commitment did not guarantee full implementation. Rather, greater site implementation progress was associated with continued design team interaction and support. Teams and school staff indicate some common elements in an effective assistance strategy:

- An introduction to the design by the team that was compelling or at least clear and that was provided to *all* staff.

- Relevant training provided to *all* administrators and teachers at the school with behavioral changes or new processes modeled.

- Concrete materials and models to use in classrooms, committees, or other forums for reform.

- Help of the design team members or presence of a school-level facilitator to aid staff in day-to-day implementation.

- Teacher-teaming to work on design issues or curriculum development.

- Participatory governance to ensure continued teacher support of the design.

- Perhaps most important, teacher time for curriculum development, teacher-to-teacher interactions, and practice at the individual and school level to become adept at new behaviors.

Barriers to Change in Schools

It was the combination of design and implementation that began to produce significant changes in the way school staff thought of their jobs and addressed the needs of students. Although not evident in every school, the end of Phase 2 saw many sites turning to the following as the means to make permanent changes to the culture of the school:

- A new vision of professionalism in which teachers take greater responsibility for all school functions and in which design teams assist or act as agents of change by providing: training; critical information systems; new forms of interactions between parents, teachers and students; and quality-control mechanisms for the delivery of curriculum and instruction, etc.

- Increased autonomy to ensure that the school has discretionary power over budget, staffing positions, and hiring and firing in keeping with the design goals.

However, by the end of Phase 2, schools noted significant barriers to the sustained professional development desired and their attempts to gain autonomy. Perhaps more significant, clashes between the culture of particular schools and those of the design teams and the inability of the teams and schools to address issues of public engagement posed potent threats to the continued efforts.

ACCOMPLISHMENT OF NASDC AS A WHOLE

NASDC encouraged the creation of nine design teams, seven of which it has chosen to go on to Phase 3. At this time, the distinctive contribution of NASDC has been to help capitalize, support, and legitimize a potential new mechanism for the building of school-level capability for transformation: a design-based assistance organization. This organization, when fully operational, will combine both design principles and a concentrated dose of training and assistance to produce a significant change in the school and student outcomes.

Lessons from the Phase 2 effort indicate that to be effective in helping transform schools, a design-based assistance organization should have the following:

- A capable design team that can provide design-related assistance to multiple sites.

- A fully developed design that communicates effectively the vision and specific tasks of school reform advocated by the team. This design should include a self-critical feedback component useful to schools in measuring their progress toward reform.

- A proven implementation strategy that allows the schools to become adept at quality control of the curriculum and instruction within the school and that helps schools change the structure of professional development, scheduling, and governance to support student education goals.

- The existence of demonstration sites to act as further laboratories of reform and to provide hands-on evidence of success.

IMPORTANT, BUT LIMITED, ROLE OF NASDC

If fully developed over the next few years, this combination of design and assistance in transforming the school might prove to be a powerful impetus toward improved student outcomes in many schools. However, it does not present the only intervention or a complete picture of needed reform efforts. The usefulness of the design-based assistance organization appears limited to school- and perhaps district-level changes. Important actors with strong systemic influence on schools remain outside these teams' and NASDC's ability to influence them. These are quasi-governmental bodies, higher-level governmental bodies, assessment organizations, teachers' colleges, schools of higher education, and the general public.

The ability of NASDC to influence change at a more systemic level will be put to the test in Phase 3 as it enters into agreements with a small group of jurisdictions to work toward school-level transformation for more than 30 percent of the district's schools within a five-year period.

ACKNOWLEDGMENTS

We would like to thank the New American Schools Development Corporation and the Ford Foundation for their support of our study of the implementation efforts of the nine design teams. This report would not have been possible without the aid and cooperation of the design teams, districts, and schools involved in the NASDC effort. People in each organization gave freely of their time to enable us to understand the issues involved in developing and demonstrating new designs for schools. We thank them for their efforts and also for their dedication to improving the educational prospects of all children. Finally, we would like to thank the many reviewers of this report who helped improve it dramatically, especially David Finegold and Georges Vernez.

ACRONYMS

AC Audrey Cohen College System of Education
AT Authentic Teaching, Learning, and Assessment
ATLAS Authentic Teaching, Learning, and Assessment of All Students
CES Coalition of Essential Schools
CLC Community Learning Centers
CON Co-NECT
CRESST Center for Research on Evaluation, Standards, and Student Testing
CSTEEP Center for the Study of Testing, Evaluation, and Education Policy
EL Expeditionary Learning
KERA Kentucky Education Reform Act
LALC Los Angeles Learning Center
LEARN Los Angeles Educational Alliance for Restructuring Now
MRSH Modern Red Schoolhouse
NA National Alliance for Restructuring Education
NASDC New American Schools Development Corporation
NCREST National Center for Restructuring Education, Schools, and Teaching
NSP New Standards Project
PLP Personal Learning Plan
RFP Request for Proposal
RW Roots and Wings
SCANS Secretary's Commission on Achieving Necessary Skills
SPMT School Planning and Management Team
TAG Talented and Gifted program

Chapter One

INTRODUCTION

This report summarizes RAND's formative assessment of the New American Schools Development Corporation (NASDC) initiative to develop and implement whole-school designs for improving student outcomes. It offers the public, especially jurisdictions and schools interested in implementing educational reform, lessons learned to date from the NASDC initiative for whole-school transformation. The report describes the context of the NASDC efforts and the methodology used for the formative assessment and contrasts the nine designs and their implementation progress toward whole-school transformation. It then explores reasons for variances in progress among teams as well as factors that affected the progress of all teams.

This chapter describes NASDC's origins and approach to school reform, provides a brief history of the NASDC efforts, describes the purpose of this RAND formative assessment report, summarizes the methodology used in the formative assessment, and outlines the remainder of the report.

NASDC's PURPOSE AND APPROACH

For many years education reformers have been frustrated over the inability to bring about school reforms that lead to improved student outcomes.[1] Letting schools innovate on their own appeared to have

---

[1]We do not provide a literature review of education reform implementation. The following would be helpful to a reader unacquainted with the field: Berman and

limited success, resulting in the adoption of marginal programs or the disappearance of improvements when a principal or sponsor changed. Imposing state and district mandates appeared to offer similarly meager successes, with programs disappearing when state and district attention wavered or funding was reduced.[2]

The nation's governors met in 1991 to develop a strategy for improving the performance of the nation's children that encouraged both systemic changes from the top and better assistance for individual schools trying to improve.[3] One initiative favored by the governors' conference was to create a privately funded effort to develop and implement whole-school designs to increase student achievement. Participants felt that school improvement failed in part because of the lack of coherent and cohesive designs for schools that avoided programmatic add-ons to already confused and fragmented policies. It was thought that new, holistic designs, created by professionals aware of the best practices, might help to completely and effectively transform existing schools to produce improved student outcomes.

In July 1991, NASDC, a private nonprofit corporation funded by the private sector, was established in conjunction with President Bush's America 2000 initiative to support design teams capable of helping existing schools transform themselves into high-performing schools that increase student performance. Later, NASDC was endorsed by President Clinton in keeping with his administration's Goals 2000.

NASDC's Purpose

NASDC's goal is increased or improved student performance. The means for achieving this is to establish school designs and teams that can lend assistance to schools in a whole-school transformation. NASDC hoped to engage the nation's best educators, business people, and researchers in the deliberate and thoughtful creation of teams that would develop and demonstrate whole-school designs

---

McLaughlin (1975), Cuban (1990), Elmore and McLaughlin (1988), Firestone et al. (1989), Smith and O'Day (1990), and Tyack (1990).

[2]The top-down versus bottom-up dilemma has been voiced before, but recently in contrasting articles by Usdan and Schwarz in *Education Week* (1994).

[3]For a review of education reform at the time of NASDC, see the special report by *Education Week* on frustrations with reforms (1993).

and go on to assist many schools across the nation in transforming themselves.[4] The idea was to contribute to the national school improvement effort by creating the capability in several organizations to provide designs that could more reliably aid whole-school transformation and by providing for the observable implementation of those designs. A major condition NASDC placed on all teams was that the designs as implemented in schools would be no more costly than normal, allowing for some additional costs associated with the transition or transformation period.

NASDC's Approach

NASDC is using a "change agent "approach to improved student outcomes.[5] As in the classic case of the U.S. Department of Agriculture, the design team as change agent brings both expertise and assistance to the potential adopters: It should affect the traditional relationships and de facto fragmented designs of existing schools by offering new and coherent designs and transformation assistance to schools seeking to reform (see Figure 1.1). This interaction between schools and a design team is expected to result in changed school policies and classroom behaviors, as well as better support of student learning through integrated social services and parental involvement. These in turn are intended to result in improved student performances—the ultimate NASDC goal.

---

[4]For a better understanding of NASDC's original intentions, see New American Schools Development Corporation (1991).

[5]"Change agent" as a concept for implementing reform gained widespread usage owing to original studies by Everett Rogers (1962) of the U.S. Department of Agriculture's community-based extension programs. It refers to the situation where a party that wishes to effect change in an organization, community, or other unit uses a third party or a subordinate to locally intervene to promote change. This local intervenor is the change agent and usually is an expert in the innovation being promoted who is locally situated to provide hands-on assistance to potential adopters. The change agent's local presence encourages a level of mutual respect and trust between the change agent and adopters. This in turn is felt to preclude some of the resistance to change exhibited when initiators of innovation are seen as outsiders. The term came into the education reform literature through the RAND "change agent study" by Berman and McLaughlin (1975), which showed how federal programs attempting education reform often failed because they were perceived to be top-down mandates.

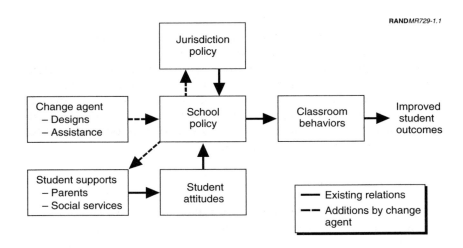

RAND*MR729-1.1*

Figure 1.1—Design Teams Act as Change Agents

NASDC intended its effort to differ in important ways from past governmental approaches.

- The effort is privately funded and supported. It is not a government program involving top-down mandates for change with associated "resistance" that has led to failure in the past.

- The premise of the effort was that no one solution would work in every school. Thus, NASDC chose to develop different design teams to promote informed choices about designs. This is a significant break with some past efforts that sought to impose on schools a single best solution from above.[6] NASDC emphasized school-level choice.

- Neither is the premise of the effort strictly bottom-up, with each school pursuing individualistic and idiosyncratic efforts. Rather, the school transformation is design-based, with coherence of school-level policies an important tenet of the initiative. NASDC's approach involves the deliberate creation of whole-

---

[6]For more about the failure of top-down reforms, see Firestone et al. (1989), and Smith and O'Day (1990).

school designs, not the addition of interesting programs to fix specific problems in schools.

- In connection with the previous item, the designs are intended to address all students' needs and are not special programs targeted on specific populations to be added to the school repertoire.

- The deliberate creation of teams to develop designs and the capacity to demonstrate and test them in real schools has not been attempted before. Other reform organizations have grown in more organic and serendipitous ways.

- NASDC emphasized that the purpose of the teams was not replication of a prescriptive design but the development of designs that could help schools meet high standards within reasonable costs by adapting designs to multiple local conditions.

- Recognizing the complexity of the task at hand, NASDC planned for several phases (shown in Figure 1.2) that match the concepts

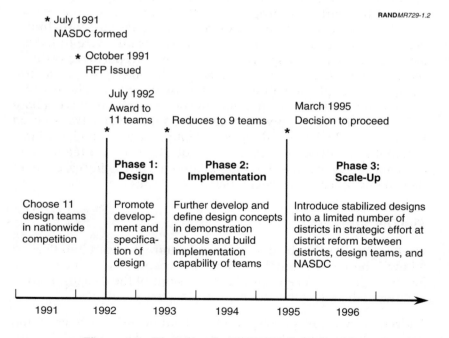

Figure. 1.2—Time Line for NASDC Reform Agenda

of diffusion described by Rogers (1962). In the development and testing phase, design teams could work on their concepts with a small number of real schools that were likely to be risk-takers. In a subsequent scale-up phase, the teams, more experienced and adept at assistance, would enter new sites that would have less inclinations toward innovation. The accomplishments of NASDC, and whether the designs can be adopted by schools to increase student performances, will be apparent only at the end of the scale-up phase.

NASDC HISTORY

In the past three years, NASDC has evolved through two of its phases.

Phase 1

A year after its creation, following a request for proposal (RFP) that resulted in nearly 700 proposals, NASDC announced that it was awarding contracts to 11 teams for a year-long design effort. In this period, known as Phase 1, teams receiving awards were to further develop their teams, designs, and assistance concepts to ready themselves for entering demonstration sites. The goal was to have firm designs and implementation strategies by the end of Phase 1 that would allow the teams to enter into the demonstration sites of Phase 2. In addition, the teams were required to submit plans that showed that they could take their designs to multiple schools in Phase 3 in a national scale-up effort. At the end of Phase 1, two teams were dropped largely because they did not present convincing cases about their ability to scale up beyond their existing sites.

The Design Teams

Brief descriptions of the designs that did move forward into Phase 2 follow. These teams are the subject of this study. We note that the following statements encapsulate the visions of the designs, not the realities of their demonstration.

Audrey Cohen College System of Education (AC). A holistic and purpose-driven curriculum is the centerpiece of the design. This interdisciplinary, applied learning curriculum focuses on the purposes of learning and leads students through a series of constructive social actions. All associated activities in the school change to support the learning purposes. For grades K–12.

ATLAS (Authentic Teaching, Learning, and Assessment of All Students) Communities (AT). The design requires a participatory governance structure focused on a K–12 feeder pattern (pathway). Although it has strong principles of interdisciplinary curriculum and instruction, the unique focus is on the consensus-building governance needed to lead away from fragmented, bureaucratic learning environments to unified support for a community of learners. For grades K–12.

Community Learning Centers (CLC). The design requires that schools have an "institutional bypass" from the current system of regulations that bind school-level improvement. The core of the school is a personal learning plan for each student to promote individualized instruction with continuous assessment of student and school progress. The school becomes the community center for education, social, and health services. For grades K–12.

Co-NECT Schools (CON). School-based design teams tailor a generic design to meet local needs. With district and community support, the local design is implemented, and continuously refined, by teams of empowered, accountable teachers. Modern technology, featuring desktop Internet participation, supports a project-based curriculum and continuous assessment of school and student progress. For grades K–12.

Expeditionary Learning Outward Bound (EL). Dedicated to complete development of students and teachers by extending the values of Outward Bound into schools, the curriculum and instruction are transformed into expeditions of learning intended to develop intellectual, physical, and civic skills of students. Teachers become guides and participate in continuous, innovative professional development. For grades K–12.

Los Angeles Learning Center (LALC). A unique partnership of the district, teachers' union, universities, businesses, and community groups committed to overcoming urban distress and jointly building a school of the future dedicated to individual support. Emphasis is placed on strong social support for students within the school and community. For grades K–12.

Modern Red Schoolhouse (MRSH). The design blends elements of traditional education with new instructional methods to provide all students with a strong foundation in American culture as well as skills needed for future employment. For grades K–12.

National Alliance for Restructuring Education (NA). An alliance of states, districts, schools, and expert organizations created to effect system change at all levels by promoting ambitious standards and accountability mechanisms. The design uses results-based high-performance management at the school and district levels with de-centralized decisionmaking to restructure the learning environment to support student achievement and provides professional support to teachers and schools. For grades K–12.

Roots and Wings (RW). A relentless and organized approach to en-suring that all children leave elementary school with the skills required for success. The design reallocates existing federal, state, and local resources into a system of curriculum, instruction, and family support designed to eliminate special education and low achievement. For grades K–6.

Phase 2 and Its Goals

In July 1993, NASDC awarded nine teams two-year contracts to demonstrate their designs in two or more schools. The nine design teams developed and refined their concepts in 147 schools in 19 states through June 1995. NASDC's goals for Phase 2 were straight-forward—the finalization of the designs and demonstration of all el-ements of the designs in the sites. Specific goals for the design teams included:

- Finalize the designs in documents and other materials to pro-mote easy understanding and implementation.

- Show full demonstration of all elements of the design in the sites to prove that the designs are implementable.

- Refine implementation strategies and assistance to ensure the ability to scale up and become independent entities in Phase 3.

- Provide some indication that the designs as implemented in the demonstration sites improved student performance.

We note here that there is no literature on education reform that would support the view that these objectives could be obtained in the time period provided, no matter how much money or effort is put into school transformation. Some evidence exists that specific programs can be put in place within this timeframe, but no studies we are aware of show that whole-school transformation can be accomplished in short order. On the contrary, the experience of other reform efforts geared to whole-school transformation indicates that it takes a minimum of five years, if it can be accomplished at all.[7] As Adelman and Pringle (1995) indicate, "the process of school reform has taken more time than was initially allocated to it." NASDC decisionmakers were aware of these concerns from the beginning but felt that the ambitious deadlines would encourage due diligence.

Phase 3

In June 1995 the nine teams were reduced to seven after NASDC's internal evaluation of the capability of the teams to meet the goals of Phase 3—multiplying efforts to many sites to help more schools transform. NASDC dropped the CLC and LALC teams from its Phase 3 expansion efforts but remains supportive of them in their local efforts in Minnesota and Los Angeles. This reduction was based largely on assessments of whether the teams had developed the potential for further widespread scale-up.

PURPOSE OF RAND FORMATIVE ASSESSMENT REPORT

The strong business backing provided to NASDC and its founding in the public debate concerning America 2000 ensured that public accountability would be a major NASDC concern. As part of this effort

---

[7]Other school-level transformation activities allow schools a longer period of time to demonstrate changes. Levin (1993) states, "It takes about six years to fully transform a conventional school to accelerated status." Prestine and Bowen state (1993, p. 302) in writing on the Coalition of Essential Schools, "a minimum of five years was recommended for the entire process." See also Herman and Stringfield (1995) and Policy Studies Associates (1994).

to be responsive to public scrutiny, NASDC has promoted continuous assessment of the design teams' efforts. It asked RAND to perform part of the analytic support needed to provide both internal information for making decisions and public information about progress. It asked RAND to:

- Provide a formative assessment of the design teams' efforts against the NASDC goals for Phase 2 and draw lessons learned from the Phase 2 experience that might be useful for Phase 3 or for assessing the contribution of the whole-school, change agent approach to school improvement.

- Track the costs associated with the teams in terms of what schools would have to pay for reform.[8]

- Build the capability to formally evaluate the outcomes associated with schools in Phase 3.[9]

This report addresses the first task: Provide a formative assessment of the experience of Phase 2 and draw lessons learned. Because it is an early assessment, it can provide useful information to all involved about how to improve the process so as to better ensure the final desired outcome of increased and improved student performances.

A large school reform literature indicates that a major problem in school reform is not that the interventions do not have the desired effects but that the interventions are never implemented as proposed so as to have the desired effects (Berman and McLaughlin, 1975; Cuban, 1990; Elmore and McLaughlin, 1988; Firestone et al., 1989). Recognizing this, the purpose of Phase 2 is to develop designs and demonstration sites to the point where the interventions are in place—if not fully stable—and effects could be expected.

The question to be addressed in this report precedes the more formal evaluation of student outcomes: Did the teams actually put in place the interventions they proposed that they believe would ultimately

---

[8]This will be the topic of forthcoming RAND research by Randy Ross.
[9]Mitchell (1995).

end in improved student outcomes? Once this is established and time allowed for effects to occur, evaluations of the effects of the interventions can take place. Thus, the assessment is formative in two senses: (1) It focuses on early issues of whether the designs themselves have been developed and implemented so as to have a probable effect on student outcomes, and (2) it deals only with the early stages of the transformation process in schools, when changes in student outcomes are not expected.[10] Although this is a "final" report on Phase 2 efforts, it is not a final report on the NASDC effort.

Design teams are responsible for their own student outcome evaluations during Phase 2. Given the short period of time—two years in which to make an observable effect in a school—and the developmental changes expected in the designs, we imagine that these evaluations will not be compelling. On the other hand, evaluations of the Phase 3 efforts, when designs have stabilized and teams are capable of implementing them, would make more sense and are expected to show more compelling evidence for support or nonsupport of future design team efforts.

The report addresses several questions and is organized into chapters that respond to each question:

- What were the essential characteristics and differences among the designs and teams at the beginning of Phase 2?

- How did these characteristics and differences affect progress toward NASDC Phase 2 goals?

- Did the teams develop effective implementation and assistance strategies for whole-school transformation in line with NASDC goals for Phase 2?

- Were there important institutional, cultural, or systemic barriers to reform that need to be addressed to improve the effort?

- Given the answers to the above questions, what has been the collective contribution of NASDC to reform so far?

---

[10]Walter Williams (1975) refers to this as an implementation analysis.

METHODS

This section describes the methods used to track design team progress at sites toward implementation of the designs. Further information, especially concerning criteria for assessment, is covered in Chapter Three and Appendix B.

Case Study Approach

The phenomenon to be studied is the model of change adopted by NASDC—the creation and intervention of an entity called a design team to promote school reform. The phenomenon includes the development of the teams as well as their experiences in demonstrating their designs. This highly complex process lends itself to case study analysis. The evidence sought is qualitative—actors' descriptions and assessments of their experiences and barriers to their desired actions. We rely entirely on the differences among the teams and their sites to provide the contrasts to be studied.

Unit of Analysis and Choice of Sites

The design team and its design are considered the unit of analysis, resulting in nine cases. We expect the relationships of each design to its demonstration sites to be unique and to offer interesting insights. Therefore, the subunit of analysis will be the school or district (when appropriate as the design team's intervention point).

For each team we have chosen two schools or districts to study. For example, the CON design has chosen to work in two schools in two districts. These two schools form the basis for observations about the ability of the team to demonstrate its design in real schools. However, the AT design's construct is a feeder pattern of schools (referred to in their design as a pathway) including the elementary schools, middle schools, and common high school that serve a geographic area. The unit of analysis for this team is the pathway consisting of several schools. Thus, for AT we chose two pathways to study, each pathway including several schools.

The sample includes urban and rural schools and districts; elementary schools, middle schools, and high schools; poor schools and not-so-poor schools. Indicators for the sample are provided in Table B.1.

We note that our sample choice posed greater potential problems for two teams, CLC and NA, than for other teams. One site we chose for CLC was a tribal school that was under an administration in the throes of change and in a very dynamic economic environment. The other was a newly created charter school under the Minnesota charter legislation serving an inner-city neighborhood. Both faced potential environmental difficulties beyond those expected of other schools in the sample. For NA, our sample of five schools in three districts and our greater focus on the school level rather than the district level might have underestimated its effect, given its choice of 80 schools and greater focus on systemic change at the jurisdiction level. The effects of our sample choices became clearer over time with hindsight.

Tracking Data Elements over Time

A key theme in RAND's analysis is an examination of the evolution of the designs through time and the reasons for changes to the designs or planned progress. The initial proposals and specified NASDC goals for Phase 2, captured above, constitute the starting point. The designs evolved through Phase 1 and through Phase 2. We are interested in documenting the changes that occurred and the reasons for them.

Whole-school designs potentially incorporate a number of elements. These elements can be used to contrast and compare designs and also as a means to follow changes in designs over time. These elements are related to Goodlad's (1984) notion of school commonplaces or characteristics of schooling that are evident in all schools, even though the specific dimensions of those commonplaces might vary among schools. So, for example, all schools have a curriculum, a governance structure, and a way to determine how students are progressing, but the details of these elements vary among schools. Elements are basically ways to define the organization called school and the process called schooling.

We modified the Goodlad commonplaces after a content analysis of the design documents to fit the NASDC designs, and we now use a unique set of elements to describe, compare, and contrast the NASDC designs. The elements used in this analysis follow in brief form. We note that the definitions used are broad. This is to allow for the great variance among designs in the details of the generic elements.

- **Curriculum and Instruction**—Curriculum usually refers to the knowledge bases and the sequence in which they are covered, whether defined by traditional subject areas or in more interdisciplinary fashion. Instruction refers to the manner in which knowledge is acquired by the student and the role of the teacher in this process. In a constructivist classroom, the curriculum and instruction are determined more by the individual student than dictated by the teacher or adults, whereas in traditional classrooms the curriculum and instructional practices are often highly prescribed by adults and applied uniformly to all students. In either classroom type, curriculum and instruction together cover the heart of the interrelationship between the student, the teacher, and an understanding of the world.

- **Standards**—The range of skills and content areas a student is expected to master to progress through the system and levels of attainment necessary for students or schools to be judged effective.

- **Assessments**—The means for measuring progress toward standards, either by the schools or by students.

- **Student Grouping**—The criteria or basis for assigning students to classes, groups, or programs.

- **Community Involvement/Public Engagement**—The ways parents, businesses, and others participate in schools and vice versa.

- **Integration of Social Services**—The process of delivering social services to students to prepare them for learning.

- **Governance**—The distribution of authority and responsibility among education actors: states, districts, school members, and others. *School* governance changes usually increase the number and types of people represented in the internal decisions of the school. *District* governance changes refer to moves to site-based management and increased autonomy at the school level. *State* governance changes mandate new legal responsibilities among schools, districts, and noneducation partners.

- **Professional Development**—This has several components as discussed in team documents. Staff training includes the traditional workshops and inservices provided on particular subjects or issue areas such as cooperative learning. They are highly specific and time-constrained. Professional growth opportunities include opportunities to develop curriculum and instruction, to develop expertise in using standards, collaborate with others, and enter into networks or prolonged discussions with other teachers about the profession. Several teams planned to supplement the above two types of professional development with opportunities for changed practice, such as extensive on-the-job practice, coaching in the classroom, teaming in individual classrooms, and schoolwide forums, to permanently change the ways teachers deliver curriculum and instruction.

- **Staff and Organization**—The configuration or roles and responsibilities of different staff. Changed organizational structures and incentives can encourage teachers to access both staff inservices and professional growth opportunities.

Data Sources and Timing

We used many sources for information and many types of information:

- Background materials such as school reports, district data on conditions in the schools, newspaper reports, etc.

- Documents produced by NASDC, the teams, and schools describing their purposes and efforts.

- Interviews with important actors including design team members, parents in governing committees, lead or master teachers, site coordinators and facilitators, school administrators, district administrators, and state administrators.

- Group interviews of students, teachers, parents.[11]

---

[11]The designs intend to affect all teachers and all students at the school level. To reach as many of these actors as possible, we chose to use group interview techniques. Group interview protocols were developed to elicit group views on issues involved in implementation and progress toward design team goals. This technique's strength is that it provides in-depth coverage of issues and personal experiences and allows for adaptation to the circumstances of particular designs and sites. However, its weakness is that it does not provide the statistical data of a survey. A survey instrument,

- Observation of school activities and a limited number of classes.

This information was gathered in three waves: fall 1993 site visits, spring 1994 site visits, and spring 1995 site visits. Each site and team was visited three times during Phase 2. The last visit corresponded to the end of Phase 2. In addition, RAND staff attended summer workshops held by teams and conferences when appropriate.

Progress Toward Goals

Part of the our formative assessment was similar to a program audit. The elements were used as the basis of audit, and changes in the elements at the site level were tracked over time.

Design Team Elements and Goals. A major premise of our work is that, because of significant differences among the designs, the progress of each team must be understood in terms of the goals and vision of the particular design. The goals and visions of each team were determined by a document review and an extended interview with the design team. In this interview we established the elements of the design, what the schedule for change was, and what progress had been made from the team's point of view.

Agreements between the design teams and NASDC call for documentation of products and processes in a series of deliverables with an agreed-upon schedule. NASDC expected the teams' efforts to culminate in the meeting of its goals for Phase 2, as ambitious as they might be. This schedule states when many elements, but not all, would be specified or documented, when they would be introduced through initial training, when pilot projects might begin, when additional training or materials would be delivered, and when elements would be fully implemented in sites. For example, in one design the schedule specifies that the reading and math curricula for certain grades will be delivered by a specific date. Teachers will be trained on a subsequent date and the curricula will be used across the appropriate grades by a further date. These agreements produced a set of expectations for an implementation audit embedded in the delivery of documents, training, pilot projects, or other actions that could

---

however, could not elicit the depth of exploration required, nor could it be modified for over 30 different schools.

be tracked as well as steps toward implementation that could be easily observed.

Implementation of a few elements was not easily tracked this way. For example, several teams included in their proposals significant re-configuration of staffing as part of the design, but specific milestones and deadlines do not appear in the schedule. In these cases, we continued to track progress on the element and to look for indications of progress after discussion with design teams as to what to expect.

Site Progress Toward Goals. At the site level, we relied on two types of evidence of progress. First, we looked for unobtrusive evidence of implementation in keeping with the schedule and expectations provided by the team. These included, but are not limited to, the existence of design team materials in the schools such as new standards documents, new assessment tools, and curriculum frameworks; establishment by the school of design-required governing committees and regularly established meetings; products from those committees such as graduation exhibitions or documents aligning curriculum across grade levels; creation of new roles and assignment of personnel such as facilitators; curriculum units developed by teachers or by the team; changes in student assignments required by the design; new technology or new configurations of technology in the school; etc.

Second, we interviewed district- and school-level staff to understand their views of the design and how much they had changed their behaviors. We asked how much their jobs had changed so far in relation to where they understood the design to be taking them, about their relationships with the teams, whether the support they needed for transformation was forthcoming, and if feedback mechanisms existed.

If evidence provided by the document review, staff interviews, and unobtrusive observation was in keeping with the expectations the design team had laid out in its agreement with NASDC for progress toward full implementation, then we assessed that the team and its sites were making progress toward implementation. We assigned three different levels of progress depending on the evidence (see

Chapter Three) and attempted through the interviews to understand what contributed to different levels of progress.

ORGANIZATION OF THE REPORT

This report is divided into chapters addressing the questions posed above. Chapter Two summarizes the essential characteristics and differences among the designs that were evident at the beginning of Phase 2. Chapter Three provides more detail about the criteria we used for gauging design team progress and indicates general levels of progress made. Chapter Four explains how the nature of the design and development approach affected the progress made by the design teams toward accomplishing their goals at the school level. Chapter Five then analyzes the implementation strategies of the teams and their effect on progress. Chapter Six discusses several reform components that either proved key in moving schools toward full transformation or proved remarkably elusive, preventing full transformation within Phase 2. The final chapter draws lessons learned and explores the contribution of NASDC so far.

Appendix A provides a synopsis of each of the designs, following the element list used in the body of this report. Appendix B provides more details on the assessment methodology.

Chapter Two

ESSENTIAL CHARACTERISTICS OF AND DIFFERENCES AMONG TEAMS AND DESIGNS

In earlier work for NASDC describing the designs and design teams, based on content analysis of their documents and interviews with the teams, we noted numerous differences among designs.[1] At a detailed level, this included such differences as whether a design team advocated multi-year or multi-age classrooms, what percentage of the curriculum would become interdisciplinary, what standards would be adopted, and what type of participatory governing structure was advocated.[2]

However, experience over Phase 2 has shown that differences beyond specific design characteristics were more important in distinguishing the teams and their likely performance. These more significant differences are described below. They are a means for the reader to become more acquainted with the designs as well as the means for setting up interesting contrasts in progress made and the reasons for those differences.

CAPACITY-BUILDING ISSUES FACING DESIGN TEAMS

The design teams did not come to NASDC equally equipped to meet the demands for rapid development, demonstration, and then scale-up. Many factors affected their readiness to undertake the NASDC effort. We draw contrasts between the teams on four factors:

---

[1]Bodilly et al. (1995).

[2]Some of these more detailed differences are outlined in Appendix A.

whether the core team was newly created with new leaders working together; whether it needed to create a staff and structure to support the effort; whether the proposal writers were the same as the developers and implementors in Phase 2; and whether the team leaders or staff had experience in implementation of school-level reform.

We summarize the standing of the different teams at the end of Phase 1. Two teams (AC and RW) began with existing organizations and a staff with proven capability to interact effectively with schools and with past school reform experience. These two teams were presented with less of a challenge in terms of needed team-building than other teams. Three other teams (CLC, CON, and NA) preexisted NASDC, had some prior experience, although not always of practical implementation in schools, but were challenged to build a staff to meet the goals of Phase 2. Four teams (AT, EL, LALC, and MRSH) faced Phase 2 with significant challenges when compared to the other teams. Each was created to respond to the RFP and so had to create a staff structure and develop leadership. AT and MRSH had considerable challenges because the proposers were not the implementors of the design. And EL and MRSH did not have prior experience at school-level reform.

NUMBER OF SITES CHOSEN

The number of sites that each team chose to work with also emerged as important. Working with many sites could possibly impose resource constraints on a team; thus, teams with a large number of sites would be more challenged to meet NASDC goals. NA distinguished itself from the other teams because it chose to demonstrate its design starting in Phase 2 in over 80 schools. By year two of Phase 2 it planned to at least double that number. It had the most ambitious number of sites. The number of sites established by the other teams ranged from 2 to 18 schools.

DIFFERENCES AMONG TEAMS IN THE DESIGN TYPE

Two characteristics capture the essence of the many differences among designs: the number and type of elements (or building blocks) included in the design and the number of collaborators that the design team would need to develop the design at a site (see Figure 2.1). Three approaches distinguish the design teams.

Core designs (AC, CON, EL, and RW) emphasize changes in elements associated with the core of schooling: curriculum, instruction, standards, assessments, student groupings, community involvement, and professional development. They focus on school-level partnerships as their main point of entry and continued interaction.

Comprehensive designs (AT, CLC, LALC, and MRSH) emphasize more elements, including integrated social services, governance changes, and organization and staffing changes, as fundamental to the design. Although these teams believe they need to construct complex collaborative efforts with groups outside schools to accomplish these goals, their main interventions are still at the school-building level.

The sole **systemic** design (NA) emphasizes changes to all elements and the need for collaboration among many partners. Rather than focusing only on the school as the intervention point, this design focuses on changing the systems that surround schools including the central office, state legislation, professional development providers, social services providers, and the community.

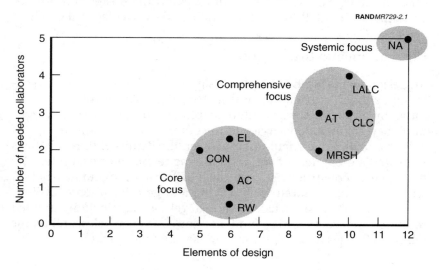

RAND*MR729-2.1*

Figure 2.1—Design Types and Collaborators Needed

Potentially, all else equal, the comprehensive designs and the single systemic one would face greater challenges in meeting NASDC Phase 2 goals than the core designs in that they pursue change in more elements of design or building blocks of the school, need to influence policies of more actors both internal and external to the schools, and intend to make changes that reform both schools and, for some, the social system surrounding schools.

The horizontal axis of Figure 2.1 deserves some further elaboration. Content analysis of the original design proposals, including updated design documents in 1994, and interviews with the teams, showed that the teams differed in the inclusion or exclusion of desired changes, reflected in the relative emphasis they put on specific elements of the design. The results, which indicate elements included in the design at the beginning of Phase 2 based on a document review and discussions with the design teams, are shown in Figure 2.2. If a team strongly emphasized an element, that is, the team said it intended to make significant changes in that building block of a "whole" school, we indicated this by using a light gray shading to show that the team is challenged to demonstrate changes in this element in the Phase 2 schools. If the team intended to demonstrate only modest changes in an element compared to that demanded by other designs, we indicate so with black. If the design did not address that element, the category is indicated with a diagonal hatch.

Curriculum and Instruction

All design teams intended to make significant changes relative to existing schools' curriculum and instruction. There was a general move by all teams toward interdisciplinary, project-based curriculum. Several included service to the community and internships as part of a required curriculum. However, the details of these changes indicated a great deal of variation among teams. For example, CLC took a very "constructivist" approach to curriculum and instruction with a student-centered view playing a large role, whereas RW favored, at least on the surface, a more developed curriculum intended to match the existing Maryland standards. Nevertheless, all teams felt that changes in these two elements were fundamental.

RAND*MR729-2.2*

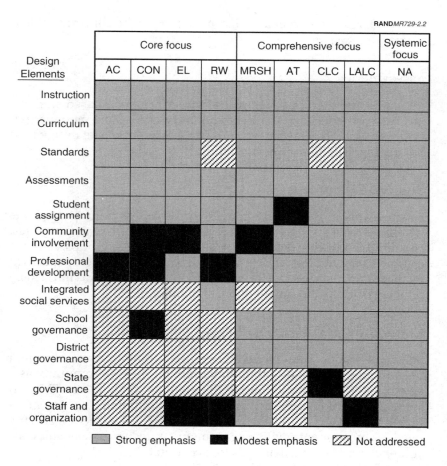

Figure 2.2—Level of Initial Challenge to Design Teams Keyed to Number of
Elements Included

Standards

Seven teams intended to create new standards of one type or another. Two designs (CLC and RW) intended to bring all students to
existing state standards. Two teams (AC and MRSH) intended to create their own unique standards, and others wanted to combine exist-

ing standards and particular skills to emphasize the concerns of their teams.

Assessments

All teams intended to develop at least performance-based student-level assessments keyed to their standards, curriculum, and instruction. Several talked about systems of assessments. The designs did not distinguish themselves further.

Student Assignment

Seven teams emphasized changes in the assignment of students within schools such as multi-age grouping, multi-year groupings, cooperative learning, and project-based learning in groups. The exceptions were AC and AT. However, although not explicitly specified by those two teams, some form of assignment change was implied by their curriculum and instructional methods.

Community Involvement/Public Engagement

Six teams emphasized the need for greater community involvement in the school or greater school involvement in the community as a key thrust of the design. For the three others (CON, EL, and MRSH) some degree of community involvement was noted, but was not a major emphasis. As designs developed, all teams recognized the need for more adept public engagement strategies to deal with constituencies and media demands for accountability.

Professional Development

Six teams stated that they intended to make fundamental changes to the professional development process for teachers as part of their designs, often including changes to the role of teachers and to teacher education. Two other teams (AC and RW) did not indicate fundamental changes to the process; rather, they indicated that professional development would change to emphasize significant training in their particular methods.

Integrated Social Services

Five teams emphasized the provision of integrated social services for students (AT, CLC, LALC, NA, and RW). AT, CLC, LALC, and NA viewed the school as the focus of provision, integrating education and social services. RW included a family support coordinator at the school but did not require the school to provide integrated social services.

School Governance

Five teams (AT, CLC, LALC, MRSH, and NA) required formal changes to school-level governance—usually the setting up of governance committees with participation of teachers and others. CON promoted the creation of two committees as desirable, but this was not required. Others encouraged these types of changes, but did not require them.

District Governance

Five teams required formal and very significant changes to the relationship between the school and district (AT, CLC, LALC, MRSH, and NA). These changes dictated school-level control over resources, budgeting, and staffing. The other teams promoted and encouraged such control, but did not require it.

State Governance

One team (NA) sought changes at the state level to promote reform, including formal changes to the responsibilities of the education and social service agencies. CLC implied state-level support for charter schools, but this was not a prerequisite for noncharter school districts in its sample.

Staff and Organization

Three teams emphasized the need for significant, permanent changes to the staff structure, and in fact based their designs on these changes (CLC, MRSH, and NA). Three others saw this as a possibility but did not require it, or they asked for the addition of a single facilitator (EL, LALC, and RW).

We note that although there were differences among teams in elements covered, all teams had two things in common. First, all took a whole-school approach. The difference among them in terms of elements covered often amounted to where to draw the line between where the school left off and other organizations began. Second, when designs were viewed as a whole, the changes envisioned were all what Cuban (1988) argues are second-order reforms directed toward fundamental change, not cosmetic improvements to the existing school.

DIFFERENCES AMONG TEAMS IN APPROACHES TO THE CHOICE BETWEEN FURTHER TEAM OR SITE-LEVEL DEVELOPMENT OF THE DESIGN

Interviews with the design teams and a review of the proposals indicated that all had given thought to the dilemma they faced concerning the relative responsibility of the team and the sites in further specification and development of the design. All teams talked in terms of organizational change being more likely if a flexible, mutual adjustment process was used. They avoided highly prescribed designs or mandatory styles of implementation. All teams used at least some aspects of a prototype development where the design was expected to evolve as the schools and design teams responded to each other and moved together toward improved levels of performance. Each team talked of its design unfolding or evolving with practical experience.

Although a common approach was apparent, at least when compared to some past top-down reform efforts, the teams tended to cluster around three, not sharply distinct, development strategies that determined the relationships between teams and sites.

Team-Developed Designs

Two teams (AC and RW) relied on the capabilities of the design teams to further develop the design. Although they worked with schools to further develop the designs through feedback, these teams intended to take major responsibility for providing the curriculum frameworks, models of lessons plans, list of resources, and models for student assignment and assessments in keeping with the specific elements of the design.

Extensive Site-Based Development

In contrast, another set of teams (AT, CLC, and NA) provided only a few specifics and general guidelines or processes of change to the schools. The schools then develop their own local designs in keeping with general guidelines. The schools develop a vision of what they will become, develop their own curriculum, and choose what kind of student groupings are appropriate. AT specified a governance structure to be followed and NA specified standards and assessments to be met and used in its results-oriented process of change. CLC relied most heavily on site-based development. This is in part because of the principles of constructivism that lay at the heart of the CLC design and that were applied equally to all actors in the school.

More Limited Site-Based Development

A final group of teams (CON, EL, LALC, and MRSH) took major responsibility in specifying the design, but relied on the sites to further develop some elements, at least in Phase 2. In common, each relied on the sites to develop curriculum and instructional models following team-developed standards, and to implement student assignment models specified by the team.

Local variation should be expected in all designs, but all else equal, the designs with greater reliance on site-based development faced potentially more challenges for Phase 2. Greater reliance on sites for local development put the ability of the teams to demonstrate progress under the direct influence of sites and site-level capability, especially in the areas of curriculum and instruction development. If sites did not promote the designs and assign time and resources to development, these teams would not show as much progress as those associated with team-developed designs. On the other hand, team-developed designs might be subject to some setbacks if the sites did not like the developed design provided to them.

RESOURCES FOR DESIGN TEAM DEVELOPMENT AND FOR SCHOOL TRANSFORMATION

None of the report's discussion addresses a potentially important difference among designs that could challenge their ability to develop and implement at sites within Phase 2: funding levels. The design teams received different amounts of funding for their own development and provided different amounts of funding to sites for implementation. On the face of it, the absolute amount of funding a team received could be an important challenge, but one cannot make that assumption because of confounding factors. This deserves to be explored a little more.

The NASDC awards given to design teams for Phase 2 activities ranged from just under $2 million to $5 million per year. These awards were to be used as the teams chose. Previous discussion indicated that teams intended different types of reforms, entered different numbers of sites, and had varying levels of capacity already developed. To develop a design might require extensive investment in one area, say standards and assessment, but not in another. For example, MRSH decided to develop its own set of standards, whereas RW adopted the Maryland standards. The two teams had significantly varied workloads in this regard. Therefore, a priori, one could not expect the absolute dollar amount of the award to a design team to indicate its implementation progress in schools, without significant understanding of its workload.

On the other hand, the design teams intended that some of their NASDC funding go directly to their sites to buy services, materials, professional development days, computers, etc. The amount going to sites varied among design teams from approximately 20 percent of their NASDC funding to close to 60 percent. This level of funding provided directly to schools for implementation potentially would have a more immediate effect on school-level implementation progress.

However, our analysis shows that a direct correlation is also not likely because of several factors.[3] First, funding to schools provided

---

[3]Ross, in forthcoming work, will document the range of levels of resources available to different schools and how that affects the funding needed to implement a design.

by design teams was often based on existing resources in the school. For example, schools associated with some teams received varying dollar amounts for the purchase of additional computer equipment depending on what already existed in the school. For one design team, district A might give the schools 10 days of professional development time, but district B might provide only four. The team might thus have given funding for more professional development to the school in district B. Second, the schools varied in their relative progress toward the design reforms before association with a team. For example, some schools might already have had training on multi-year and multi-age groupings and converted classrooms to this configuration. Their need for further training or equipment would be less than that in other schools. Finally, the schools that received large sums of money often used it to purchase computer equipment or to rewire the school and improve access to computer services. These would have only a very indirect affect on the implementation of many of the elements. For example, funding for computers would not indicate progress on standards and assessment, integrated social services, or new governance.

In summary, we do not track total funding amounts to design teams or schools because it does not indicate the challenge of implementation in Phase 2. More detailed analysis, not possible in the confines of this study, would perhaps show some correlation if it tracked both the amount schools needed and the amount available from all sources. This was not possible.

However, we did not drop resources per se from our analysis. Instead, resource issues tend to be embedded in discussions of other elements. If teachers did not receive professional development days as desired, we note this as a factor in implementation. If the school did not have funds for the provision of a facilitator, we note this. Our focus is on what needed to be bought, rather than on the price or funding sources. Ross, in forthcoming work, will document the final costs of implementing the developed designs for Phase 3 adopters and the potential variance in costs among sites with different characteristics.

Interestingly, the original change agent study (Berman and McLaughlin, 1975) showed no correlation between funding levels and implementation. No other studies we know of have effectively tracked the potential correlation.

IMPLEMENTATION STRATEGIES

Another area of potential contrast among the designs and teams that we could have addressed in this chapter is the implementation strategies proposed. However, with one exception, initial interviews and document reviews did not indicate enough thought on this important issue upon which to base contrasts. As already discussed, the teams differed in the amount of site-based development needed to implement their designs. Otherwise all teams intended to use extensive training, materials, etc., to ensure that the school understood and adopted the design. Several intended to use facilitators or coaches to ensure an on-site presence (AC, CON, and RW); others intended to use a trainer or lead-teacher model (AT and NA). Rather than develop any typologies in this regard, we decided to track what teams did at the sites and how the implementation strategies evolved.

IMPLICATION OF COMBINING THE CHALLENGES FACED BY TEAMS

The capacity-building challenges, numbers of sites, type of design, and demonstration approach combined into four groupings that distinguished the designs and teams at the beginning of Phase 2 and implied unique sets of challenges in meeting NASDC goals:

- AC and RW were both core designs with team development approaches. Neither team faced significant team capacity-building or site challenges when compared to others.

- CON and EL were also both core designs, but they required shared development between the team and sites. Although CON had some team capacity issues to address, EL had significantly more than most other teams, as it was newly created and had significantly less experience as a team in school-level reform.

- AT, CLC, LALC, and MRSH were comprehensive designs requiring some team and site-based development. AT and CLC required more site development than most other teams. In addition, AT, LALC, and MRSH faced significant challenges to team-building in Phase 2.

- Alone, NA was a systemic design requiring significant site-level development. Having few challenges to team-building, its greatest challenge was to produce significant change in over 80 schools and their associated districts and states.

Chapter Three

RELATIVE PROGRESS TOWARD IMPLEMENTATION

This chapter describes the means and criteria we used to assess progress toward the NASDC goal of full implementation by the end of Phase 2 of all elements of a design. It then summarizes the findings across teams.

CRITERION FOR ASSESSMENT OF IMPLEMENTATION PROGRESS

We used the NASDC Phase 2 goal of full implementation of all elements of the design as the criterion for this formative assessment. Failure to meet the NASDC goal of full implementation cannot be interpreted as failure to reform or failure of the efforts of the design team, but only as failure to fully comply with NASDC expectations. A highly successful effort by other standards would not meet the NASDC goals. Other school-level transformation activities allow schools a longer period of time to demonstrate changes.

There is no easy way to summarize progress made within an element and there certainly is no rubric to summarize progress across elements for a design. The latter we did not attempt. For the former we used informed judgment structured by an audit-type format that tracked each element and the expected progress. We tried to be consistent in our approach and double-checked our findings with the design teams in a letter and conference call after each site visit. In this report we summarize our assessment using three levels of progress:

Beginning progress: Concepts and models had been developed and documented by the design team; sites had been introduced to these concepts through initial training sessions; pilot programs were in place serving a minority of the school population and involving a minority of the teachers. If a element of the design had not been developed, then the team was assigned this level of progress.

Moderate progress: Pilots were being adopted by more teachers as their success was demonstrated; more in-depth training on specific issues was provided; quality control of the curriculum and instructional delivery was initiated, with teachers beginning to use standards and rubrics to determine levels of student performance; the team and sites were beginning to modify the models and practices based on experience with implementation. Considerable variation in progress across sites is expected.

Substantial progress: A majority or all students and teachers are affected by the adoption of the designed element; site infrastructure, such as scheduling, teacher evaluation methods, staffing positions, and planning, is changed to support the institutionalization of the design; quality control of the curriculum and instruction is becoming institutionalized in new practices and standard procedures.

Little to beginning progress was quite easy to identify. For example, if a design team promised to establish its own standards by a certain date, but produced no documents and admitted to being behind in this task, then the finding was clear. When we found few teachers in any school associated with a design who could explain the design, and the team admitted it was behind schedule for introducing the design, again the finding was clear.

The more difficult area was in understanding nonuniform progress across sites. We expected, and did indeed see, great variation in demonstration among the sites associated with any given team. If steady progress was being made at some sites but not others, we looked for the reasons. If the reasons for slow progress were beyond the control of the design team or the school, then we discounted the lack of progress at the slow site. For example, we expected that newly created schools would be quite chaotic in their first year and would show less progress than established schools. A school with a new principal or one beset by preexisting teacher/management strife might also be reasonably slower to progress.

We differentiated substantial progress from moderate progress in a straightforward manner. Moderate progress was indicated when several sites were behind schedule or extensive site variation was un-explained. Alternatively, it was indicated when the team did not de-liver a final product or meet a scheduled implementation, but could show works in progress and site-level activity in the area beyond that of the beginning stages of implementation.

Substantial progress was indicated when all sample sites were con-sistent in their progress (or one or two sites were slightly behind for obvious reasons), and the progress generally met the expectation and schedule established by the team for implementation by the end of Phase 2.

Perhaps unfairly, we did not credit a design team with progress in an element when that element existed in a site before the partnership with the design team. For example, a design team's vision might in-clude multi-age and multi-year clusters. If this existed at a site be-fore its involvement with the design team, we judged that the team had neither demonstrated, nor failed to demonstrate, its capability for introducing this element into a site. We maintain that if NASDC's purpose is to create design team capability to transform schools, then the team must show this transforming capability at sites by be-ing responsible in some way for the transformation. Preexisting transformation undertaken by the school does not reflect design team capability. This is a somewhat controversial position. Others argue, with reason, that if the element exists at a site then it stands as demonstrated.

DIFFERENCES IN PROGRESS AMONG DESIGNS AND TEAMS

Over the two-year period of Phase 2, RAND tracked the progress made by the teams toward their individually stated goals within each element. These findings are summarized in Figure 3.1.

RAND*MR729-3.1*

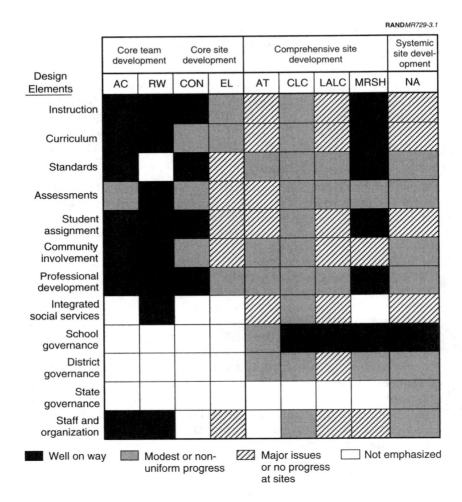

Figure 3.1—Progress Toward Goals Indicated by Design

Manifestations of Progress

The following statements provide more context for the progress marked on the figure. By the end of Phase 2, NASDC expected no less than the creation of design teams, full demonstration of the envisioned changes in elements in at least two schools, and the building of team capability for expansion in Phase 3.

- White in Figure 3.1 indicates that the team did not address this element in its original proposal; therefore, it was not challenged to demonstrate changes in the element.

- Diagonal hatches in Figure 3.1 indicates that a team did include this element but shows a comparatively low level of progress toward implementation of the concepts in the design. Implementation was at the beginning stages, with the team in the process of specifying concepts, developing models, introducing the site to the ideas through training, and establishing or running pilots. Teachers might be busily working on curriculum units, but these units had not been fully developed, reviewed for quality, or put into a scope and sequence. Outreach to external actors would be tentative at this point—establishing contact and getting regular meetings under way with actors such as social services or professional education schools. Participatory governance committees would be formed, but not yet working smoothly. Autonomy was usually provided through waivers.

- Light gray indicates that the team intended changes in this element and that progress toward full implementation was moderate, usually with varying progress across sites. At this point, the schools were moving away from pilots toward increased involvement of teachers and students. Training switched from introductory sessions describing design elements in general terms to more substantial issues of change. Quality control was initiated by reviewing curriculum units against standards and deleting or improving units to fit into an agreed-upon scope and sequence for learning across the school as a whole. Teams and sites would be refining the models and materials used. Links to outside actors would begin to be strengthened with actual changes being made in service delivery. Participatory governance would begin to affect school decisions and autonomy would be moving from waiver-based toward grants of independence based on performance.

- Black shows that the progress was in keeping with what was described by the team as the final goal for Phase 2—full implementation of the concept in at least two schools—and was fairly consistent across sites associated with the design. Most students and teachers would be affected within the schools. The infrastructure of the school would be changing to support the new design on a permanent basis and quality control would have become automatic through teacher evaluation, new assessments, etc.

We note that in all cases: (1) progress in middle schools and high schools was less than progress in elementary schools,[1] and (2) the design teams' sites, and our sample, included more elementary schools.[2] Therefore, a design team can be marked as having made substantial progress, when in fact most of that progress was evident in elementary schools and progress in an associated high school lagged.

Basic Patterns of Progress

A quick review of the findings, as displayed in the figure, indicate the following.

Within a design team, progress across elements was relatively consistent. The simplest explanation for this is that some design teams were better suited to meet the goals of NASDC than others, whether by dint of their previous experience or by the nature of their designs and approaches. Others appeared to make less progress across the board.

The two teams (AC and RW) regarded as most ready at the beginning of Phase 2 and with core designs (fewer elements) that relied heavily on team development substantially implemented most of their elements. The two other core designs with site development (CON and EL) did not implement their design elements to the same extent. Of these two, EL had the greatest challenges in terms of readiness and implemented less of its design than the other core designs.

---

[1]In several cases this was deliberate. For example, both AC and MRSH focused their initial efforts in elementary schools and delayed design development and implementation in high schools. This was understood in the contract between NASDC and the teams and in the agreed-upon progress milestones. Thus, for at least these two teams, it was understood that less progress would be seen in high schools.

[2]The sample of schools is listed in Table B.1.

In general, the comprehensive and systemic designs showed lower levels of implementation across their many elements. They did not accomplish the extent of progress exhibited by the core designs in the elements of curriculum, instruction, standards, assessment, professional development, and community involvement. The exception appears to be MRSH. Aside from school governance, these teams at best made only moderate implementation progress on the elements peculiar to their designs: governance, integrated social services, and staffing and organizational changes.

Finally, among the group of comprehensive and systemic designs with shared development, those with readiness and site challenges (AT, LALC, and NA) tended to have implemented fewer of their elements than the teams without those challenges. The exception appears to be MSRH.

The next chapter explores in more depth some of the reasons behind these findings.

Chapter Four

RELATIVE IMPLEMENTATION PROGRESS ASSOCIATED WITH DIFFERENCES IN DESIGNS OR TEAMS

This chapter analyzes one set of issues: whether and how the challenges we noted at the beginning of Phase 2 influenced progress during Phase 2, if that influence is likely to continue into Phase 3, and whether it has broader implications for reform. First, some of the reasons for differences in progress among teams toward the NASDC goals are explored in more detail: the relative capacity of teams, the number of sites chosen for Phase 2 demonstration, the nature of the design, and the nature of the team's development approach. Then, changes in designs are noted and implications for Phase 3 are drawn.

EFFECTS OF TEAM READINESS ON IMPLEMENTATION LEVELS

We saw in Figure 3.1 a general association between team readiness and the level of implementation observed in Phase 2.

- The two design teams that were most ready (AC and RW) made very significant progress.

- Three of the four teams we judged to face greater challenges in terms of initial capacity accomplished a lower level of demonstration (AT, EL, and LALC).

Interviews with the teams and the sites indicate that, in fact, the readiness of the team was a key factor in producing or not producing the full demonstration results NASDC wanted.

The AC and RW teams entered the sites one year earlier than the other teams, during Phase 1. Therefore, the sites had a longer period of time to demonstrate the design and so appear to be further along with the demonstration. This early entry into sites was associated with comparatively well-developed models because standards, curriculum, and instruction already existed in the teams' repertoires.[1] Sites said they could immediately understand and begin work on demonstration using the existing models. This in turn was said to have allowed significant early progress on curriculum and instruction.

In contrast, interviews with design teams and sites indicated that three of the four comparatively less-ready teams were heavily affected by the need to develop the design at the same time they were building team capability and capacity. AT, EL, and LALC suffered to differing degrees from the following:

- Struggles to combine existing organizations with strong cultures into a new partnership (AT and LALC).

- Difficulties in translating abstract notions into specified design concepts and implementable actions (AT, EL, and LALC).

- Difficulties in quickly building the staff needed to fully develop the design and assist the sites in implementation (AT, EL, and LALC).

- Entry into the school before the design was adequately developed resulting in confusion at the sites in the first year (AT, EL, and LALC).

In contrast to AT, EL, and LALC, MRSH relied heavily on consultants and brought them on board by the second semester of the first year. In addition, as discussed below, it borrowed heavily from existing sources to arrive at a set of standards and curriculum concepts,

---

[1]RW uses the Maryland state standards and AC has its own set of standards that do not conflict with state standards but incorporate them.

rather than developing its own from scratch. It stabilized its leadership quickly.

EFFECTS OF NUMBER OF SITES ON IMPLEMENTATION LEVELS

The number of sites selected tended to adversely affect only one team. NA, the team that took on significantly more sites than other teams, showed beginning to moderate levels of implementation across many elements at the sites observed.[2]

NA began its efforts in seven states, 25 districts, and over 80 schools. Team-level interviews in fall 1993 indicated that the team had difficulty growing fast enough to meet the demands placed upon it by so many sites. This choice of sites precluded much of the school-level "hand-holding" that some teams offered. Instead, NA provided for a small group of teachers from each school to attend conferences and bring back reform ideas to the schools. Teachers did not credit this team with strong support and specifically criticized the lead teacher model. The team had a very ambitious schedule for scale-up to more sites by the second year of Phase 2, but abandoned that in the face of slow progress across the board. In response to its Phase 2 experiences, NA will concentrate during Phase 3 on its existing sites and build its capacity to assist change.

Other teams might have been affected by the number of sites, but we could not distinguish this from other factors. In part this is because some of the designs that started out with fewer sites added sites during the second year of Phase 2.[3]

---

[2]A caveat to our findings for NA is the following. NA attempted to undertake school, district, and state reform simultaneously at over 80 sites. We concentrated our efforts on school-level changes and might have missed some of the effects of NA at other levels. In addition, we included only five schools in our sample and might have missed important developments at other sites.

[3] For example, CON started with two sites (actually K–9 schools). One in Boston was dropped by the second year, but several schools were added in two jurisdictions: Hammond, Indiana, and Juneau, Alaska. AC also added several new schools in Dade County, Florida. Four additional elementary schools in St. Mary's County, Maryland, adopted the RW model and several schools were added to EL in Dubuque, Iowa. Thus, other teams do not stand out in terms of the number of sites with the exception of LALC, which had only two schools. Team-building issues were so pervasive in LALC

EFFECTS OF DESIGN TYPE ON IMPLEMENTATION LEVELS

The level of implementation also appears to be associated with the type of design. Those with more elements (comprehensive and systemic designs) had more difficulty than core designs making substantial progress in any one element, instead they displayed lower levels of progress across more elements.

- Three of the four core designs (AC, RW, and CON) show substantial implementation in over half of the elements included in the design.

- Only one of the five comprehensive or systemic designs (MRSH) showed this much progress toward implementation. The others tended to show moderate or beginning progress across almost all their elements including those that distinguish these designs: governance, integrated social services, and staff and organization.

Progress in Core Focus Elements

Four teams (AC, CON, MRSH, and RW) stand out as having made significant progress in the elements that represent the core focus of schooling, especially curriculum, instruction, standards, assessments, and student assignment. These teams exhibited some commonality that explains this level of progress.

First, these teams, when compared to others, had existing models of curriculum, standards, and students assignment (curriculum frameworks, scope and sequences, example lesson plans, content standards by grade level, and specific new assignment patterns) that were introduced to the teachers early on. In several cases, these models or the basis for them preexisted the NASDC effort: RW's Success For All reading program and its use of Maryland state standards, AC's purpose-based curriculum's scope and sequence, the already developed materials by the Urban District Assessment Consortium, Earthwatch, and others used by CON, and MRSH's Core Knowledge for elementary levels and Advanced Placement content for high

---

that having one site in the first year and only two in the second year might have been beneficial.

school. In other cases, these models were developed during Phase 1: MRSH's final set of K–12 content and skill standards, CON's resource packages for development of curriculum units, and RW's curricular units for World Lab and Math. Other teams did not enter with strong models or chose to take time to develop their own, thereby entering schools in Phase 2 with less-concrete models and materials in hand.

Second, these teams (AC, CON, MRSH, and RW) insisted that schools immediately undertake design changes in curriculum, instruction, standards, and student assignment. For example, the student assignment changes required by both RW and CON and implied by the AC design were enacted the first year without delay in addition to the curriculum and instructional changes.

This informed obstinacy contrasts with several other design teams that decided, in the face of teacher resistance, that they were expecting too much from teachers and would proceed more slowly. For example, EL remains committed to multi-year teaching but has allowed schools to institute this at their own pace—resulting in a slow and uneven implementation within sites.

Third, in schools associated with AC, CON, MRSH, and RW, all teachers immediately began work in these areas together and the teams focused the teachers' attention on curriculum and instruction matched to standards. Although a comprehensive design, MRSH, in common with the three core designs, primarily focused teachers on curriculum units and instruction guided by standards.

The other teams with comprehensive and systemic designs diffused the focus of teachers, having them consider significant changes to governance, new forms of integrated social services, the development of new standards, or discussions of appropriate pedagogy. This broader push for change produced interesting discussions, but it often precluded a focus on immediate, observable change. For at least two designs (AT and NA), teachers were dissuaded from making substantial changes to curriculum, instruction, and student assignment until after new governance and standards had been established. Since these teams have been slow in establishing standards, these other elements have lagged.

In short, the relative ability of the three core designs and MRSH to produce significant results in these elements quickly can be attributed to their unrelenting emphasis on these areas, clear focus on producing results in these elements, and their development of concrete models to accomplish these tasks. In contrast, other teams, whether core or other types of designs, had less initial focus or did not have the "core" of solid design models to produce results quickly.

The exception for progress in core elements appears to be in assessments. All teams discouraged multiple-choice, unauthentic assessments and promoted embedded, performance-based assessments. Progress was beginning to moderate in eight of the nine teams, for several reasons.

- Assessment systems are tied to standards and curriculum. Design teams developed assessments only after establishing standards and curriculum. Because these prior elements took some time to develop, several teams simply did not address this task in Phase 2.

- Assessment systems are usually dictated by state or district regulations, especially concerning non-performance-based tests. For the most part, schools did not escape these regulations and were not free to adopt new performance-based systems (see the discussion under district governance, below).

On the positive side, several teams did make progress in instituting portfolios and individual student plans including parent/teacher/ student conferences. But this was done in addition to existing assessment regimes. A separate RAND report documents the difficulties faced by schools when transitioning between two potentially conflicting systems of assessment.[4]

The comprehensive and systemic designs did not tend to produce strong progress in the "core elements" of design, but neither did they produce strong progress in other areas. The discussion now turns to the elements uniquely attempted by the comprehensive and systemic designs.

---

[4]Mitchell (1995).

School Governance

Most of the design teams attempting changes in school-level governance (AT, CLC, LALC, MRSH, and NA) tended to describe committee structures within schools that were intended to increase teachers' input into decisionmaking at the school level or increase the diversity of representation in general—adding parents, community members, and business people to those heard. By the end of Phase 2, these committee structures had been set up and were functioning. The committees were more representative than in the past. Meetings were being held on a routine basis. Cursory review of meeting votes show a participatory character.

Interviews, however, reveal a different story, but one quite typical of these type of efforts (Bimber, 1994; Liberman et al., 1991; Policy Studies Associates, Inc., 1994; Wohlstetter, 1995). Although the committees were in place and functioning, they were not always functioning in a participatory manner with changed decisionmaking functions. Principals still held great sway in these forums and in several cases the governance committees were frankly advisory to the principal. Teachers, parents, and nonadministrators did note that meetings were becoming more participatory as they learned more about the job of governing a school and the administrators learned better how to "let go."

Respondents noted that the function or focus of the committees was as important as the level of participation. Two teams received particularly positive comments in this regard: MRSH and NA. Both imposed a committee structure on the schools that corresponded to tasks each design team thought were most important. The immediate effect was to reduce the number of committees within the school to a reasonable number and to focus the school decisionmaking bodies on the design and its school transformation goals. Respondents said this construction of committees enabled the design to become the center of school attention. For NA, this new committee structure was not implemented in the schools we visited until well into Phase 2, reducing its observable effect on implementation.

District and State Governance

School autonomy from districts, the main thrust of most design teams, proved elusive. The exceptions to the following discussion are a few sites that had preexisting autonomy[5] and design teams that asked for relatively small concessions.[6]   The needed autonomy tended to lie in three areas similar to those found as definitive of site-based management (Murphy and Hallinger, 1993; Wohlstetter, 1995).

- School-level control over the entire school budget, not just discretionary funds.

- School-level control over hiring, firing, and transfer as well as creation of staff positions.

- School-level control over assessments and accountability measures used.

The successes we observed in terms of completing goals of site autonomy tended to be restricted to obtaining waivers, acting more forcefully in making school-level choices, and proper interpretation of existing regulations in favor of design teams' principles. Significant restructuring and site-based management were not obtained by the design teams but were built on preexisting changes.[7] Design teams concluded, and district officials appeared to agree, that the move toward autonomy was a process that would have to be established over time. As more schools reform, the demand for specific powers necessary to promote the design might grow and the district might begin to remove more barriers.

---

[5]For example, the NA sites in Kentucky had existing autonomy granted through the Kentucky Education Reform Act. A San Diego site for NA is a charter school under the California charter law. And several schools associated with CLC are charter schools, contract schools, or reservation schools. In each of these cases, the autonomy available to the schools preceded to a large extent the relationship with the design team.

[6]AC and RW are designated as core teams and yet have been marked as accomplishing changes in this area. However, these were very limited changes requiring the funding of one additional staff person as a school-level facilitator. This was approved in all cases. This design requirement does not match the ambitious comprehensive and systemic design requirements for full school-level autonomy over staffing decisions.

[7]Difficulties associated with restructuring and the lack of political clout of any one actor to ensure this have been described by Tyack (1990). He notes that restructuring flies in the face of a century of buildup of central office power over individual schools.

In general, the comprehensive and systemic teams attempting change in the area of school-level autonomy said:

- Most schools have the ability to innovate in terms of curriculum and instruction or can easily obtain waivers to do so, except when these innovations come in conflict with required testing regimes. All teams experienced instances where testing regimes conflicted with desired curriculum and instruction. In these instances, the teachers usually "went outside the design" to meet testing requirements.

- As outsiders, the team often lacked the political clout to affect the system of rules and regulations sufficiently to promote autonomy over budget, personnel, and staffing or assessments within the time frame of Phase 2. But within that time frame the team could build upon small successes to encourage an open dialog or negotiation between the school and the district for increased autonomy.

- The teams often lacked the local presence needed to build political influence, but existing expertise by the team could substitute for this and in several instances worked to help schools correctly interpret existing laws that stood in the way of improvements.[8]

Site-level respondents noted that:

- School staff lacked the ability to effectively use power granted in these areas because they had not been trained to do so. This was most especially felt to be the case in matters of budgeting.

- District representatives often said that many schools had been granted autonomy in these areas but did not choose to use it because of tradition or lack of competence.

- Districts were willing to grant additional school-level powers if and when schools demonstrated they could effectively use their existing powers.

---

[8]The clearest example actually comes from a core design, RW, which has on its staff nationally recognized experts on the use of federal funds. These experts could argue effectively with mid-level state and district bureaucrats for proper interpretation of federal rules. The same could be said of CLC's expertise in charter and contract schools.

Finally, we saw little effect in the Phase 2 timeframe on state-level policies for reasons similar to those for district-level changes.

Social Services

We found models of integrated social services in support of learning, associated with teams pursuing this goal, that demonstrated the concepts behind their proposals. For example, the Challenger campus associated with Prince George's County mirrors the integrated social services element described by AT. The same could be said for the JFK School Family Support Center in Kentucky and the Crawford Cluster in San Diego, both associated with NA. Neither team was responsible for these changes; they predate the presence of both teams. The only team that showed progress in this area is RW and that is because its goals were more circumscribed; it advocates additional counseling and coordination more than changed social service delivery.

Teams attempting change in this area report that the team and schools did not have the necessary contacts with social services and were not strong political players in social service provision. They are the outsiders stepping in and as such have little standing in the community of social service agencies (Smrekar, 1994).

In addition, teachers noted that when they were called upon to perform social services outreach, they did not know how to go about it and did not have the time needed to undertake it. As a result, they tended to follow familiar paths toward improvement, making only marginal changes to the existing system: advocating a school nurse position, building a stronger teacher referral system for students in need of services, etc.

Number of Elements

NASDC's goal was to have implementation of all elements in the demonstration sites. It therefore pushed teams to make progress in all elements. Thus, it should come as no surprise that in addition to problems associated with progress in certain elements, the sheer number of elements to cover posed problems for the comprehensive and systemic teams. This generally manifested itself in the team choosing to develop elements in a sequential order, putting off the more difficult school and district governance, staff and organizational changes, and integrated social service elements until after making some progress in the areas of standards, curriculum, instruction, and student assignment. Interviews with comprehensive and systemic team members indicate that the comprehensive and systemic teams, more than the core teams, were taxed to meet their stringent NASDC goals in all elements by the end of Phase 2 and that teachers felt drawn into areas where they had little expertise and little time to address overwhelming problems. Nevertheless, the teams did not drop the elements from their designs, but began to describe an "unfolding process" by which they would have to influence change and the extremely "local nature" of this process. Most often this appears to translate into an opportunistic approach toward implementation of the elements of school and district governance, staff changes, and integrated social services in which teams will build on any local efforts and take advantage of any local initiatives toward change without making stringent demands for up-front concessions.

EFFECTS OF SITE DEVELOPMENT APPROACHES ON IMPLEMENTATION PROGRESS

The approach to development, whether undertaken primarily by the design team or by the site, was also associated with teams' different level of progress.

- The two teams that provided the greatest amount of team specification and development (AC and RW) showed the most substantial progress toward demonstration. The other seven teams showed less progress across their elements.

- Three teams (AT, CLC, and NA) intended that each site be responsible for site development. Of these teams, AT and NA showed low levels of progress compared to most others.

- The LALC team intended to take a greater role in development, but the difficulties it had in developing team capability resulted in school staff taking on the role of developing the design. This design team showed progress similar to that of AT and NA.

Perhaps the easiest way to explain the effect on progress of reliance on site-based development is to explore some specific examples of how teams relied on sites for further development. The most obvious examples are in the area of curriculum development.

Site-Based Curriculum Development

The following contrasts the experiences of two teams, RW, which developed its own curriculum, and CON, which relied on teachers to develop curriculum.

RW went into its design effort with two assumptions. (1) All teachers did not have the ability to develop curriculum; only a few were very good at it. (2) Most teachers did not have the time to develop curriculum, because they were too busy teaching. Thus, RW pledged to develop its own curriculum using its own team of experts.

Over the three-year period of Phases 1 and 2, RW developed its own K–5 curriculum covering all subjects, instructional strategies, student assignment rules, and student assessment packages. It developed these using its own experts and inputs from selected teachers. This package was introduced to the schools with substantial training and coaching. The team, recognizing the possibility for teacher backlash to a "mandated" change, asked for a formal vote by teachers to accept the design before working with the school and asked that the district transfer—without penalty—any teachers who did not want to participate, if the majority of teachers voted for the design. It did not argue that the teachers should accept the package automatically because experts had developed it. Rather, the RW team argued that teachers should try it and stick to it for six to eight weeks and then give the team feedback on how to improve it. When the team received teacher feedback, this feedback was incorporated into a revised package. Teachers could point to specific changes in the curriculum that resulted from their suggested improvements. Working with the state and the district as well as teachers, the team and others are satisfied that the resulting package meets state standards and will, if properly executed, produce well-educated children.

However, the team soon found that many teachers were having difficulties with the curriculum because it covered content that they were not familiar with. The team responded by inserting a front piece to each curricular unit that reviewed the content and the needed teacher expertise and listed resources and references for the teacher to use to learn about the subject. Teachers report that this was helpful and met a real need.

At the end of the second year of Phase 2, the RW team had a package of curriculum, instruction, assessment, and student assignments matched to Maryland state standards that covers grades K–5 and provides teachers with needed content and contextual background. It was being used in all four sites. Because RW completely documents its curriculum including texts and other resources, its curriculum can be transferred to other sites as well.

In contrast, CON (in common with EL, AT, CLC, LALC, MRSH, and NA) went into the effort assuming that teachers had to develop their own curriculum because they would not use curriculum developed by others. The team thought that teachers, wanting to be creative, would embrace this task as a professional development activity.[9] The team provided resources in the form of formats, lists of books on subject areas, and time for teachers to develop their own interdisciplinary units. Teachers, working in teams, began this effort with a set of content standards, but without a scope and sequence, using their creative sense to guide them to a quality curriculum. What resulted was a set of interesting projects developed by a group of hardy teachers. Even though the team provided five weeks of time during the summer for teachers to develop curriculum, the curriculum remains unfinished, and teachers complained of the excessive time it took as well as their lack of expertise to undertake the job.

At the end of Phase 2, CON was in the process of working through a scope and sequence to integrate the units into a complete curriculum, and the quality standards of units were being reviewed. The design team argued, as did teachers, that teachers learned much from going through the process because it gave them a better appreciation of what was involved. However, all remained concerned that more units had to be developed, resources for the time involved were

---

[9]In the case of several teams, but especially CLC, this approach was also tied to a constructivist view that teachers and students would have to build curriculum together in an interactive planning process to make it meaningful.

becoming more constrained, and the existing units might not meet quality standards.

The CON scenario was better than that of most other site-based development teams (EL, AT, CLC, LALC, and NA), which depended on significant teacher curriculum development in Phase 2. The exception appears to be MRSH.

Other Site-Level Development

Imagine now the level of difficulty imposed on site capacity (time, expertise, and resources of staff) when a design team asked its sites to simultaneously develop an interdisciplinary curriculum, a new governance structure with all teachers participating, a plan for integrated social services, and student assignment plans, while providing the site with access to experts in each of these areas and perhaps days for professional development. This was the approach of AT, CLC, and NA (and, to a lesser extent, LALC because it relied on consultants to develop some elements).[10] AT also asked sites to develop their own sets of standards.[11] The site-development approach during the demonstration phase, when combined with a comprehensive or a systemic design, often resulted in reform exhaustion—teachers and staff so overextended that they were exhausted at the end of the two-year period. At the end of Phase 2, sites associated with these teams were often going through a review effort to ensure that whatever had been developed was useful and in keeping with standards or design principles.

SUMMARY OF DESIGN- OR TEAM-RELATED CHALLENGES AFFECTING PHASE 2 GOALS

A weakness of case study analysis is that it does not allow the weighing of factors against one another to determine the size of the effect of each on outcomes. Thus, we cannot say which of the factors cov-

---

[10]The approach of AT is similar to that of Coalition of Essential Schools (CES), one of its parent organizations. The literature evaluating CES has found problems related to reliance on sites for development without providing clear models or materials. See Herman and Stringfield (1995).

[11]This approach is also similar to that of the CES.

ered were most important in a team's ability to produce results. We can say that when these factors were added together, they tended to explain much of what we saw at sites.

- AC and RW are both core designs with team development approaches. Neither team faced significant readiness or site challenges compared to others. They made substantial progress in demonstrating more elements than other teams.

- CON and EL are also both core designs, but they required shared development between the team and sites. Although CON had some readiness issues to address, EL had significantly more than most other teams. These two teams made less progress than the other two core designs, with EL being substantially affected by the requirements to build team capacity.

- AT, CLC, LALC, and MRSH are comprehensive designs requiring some team and site-based development. AT and CLC required more site development than most other teams. In addition, AT, LALC, and MRSH faced significant challenges to team-building in Phase 2. Three of these teams (AT, CLC, and LALC) showed only beginning or moderate progress in most elements. MRSH stands as an exception in this analysis.

- Alone, NA is a systemic design requiring significant site-level development with the additional challenge of producing change in over 80 schools. It showed beginning or moderate progress in most elements.

CHANGES TO DESIGNS

The implications of the above in measuring differences between design types have been moderated because of a phenomenon that began to emerge by the end of Phase 2. Core designs were beginning to add the elements that had once distinguished the comprehensive and systemic designs and several site-development designs began to move away from that strategy. The latter change made it unclear whether the initial emphasis on site development was sometimes adopted because of lack of readiness or because of a true philosophical commitment to that approach.

Addition of Elements to Core Designs

Even though the core designs did not originally intend to change district governance or social services, by the end of Phase 2 they found the designs could not be maintained in schools that did not have discretion from the district over some budget and personnel decisions and did not seek out ways to better prepare children for learning. A few examples will help to explain what happened.

The CON design relies heavily on computers for curriculum and instructional delivery, student assessment tracking, school records management, and for the interaction among disparate groups within the CON network of schools. Its successful development of new learning contexts depends on computer support. It also depends on a substantially higher number of computers in schools and extensive training of teachers in new methods of instruction and assessment. During Phase 2, the CON team recognized that it would not be able to work with schools that did not have (1) access to substantial investment dollars for computers, (2) access to funds for computer technicians, and (3) significant opportunities for professional development days not provided by the team. The obvious answer to these needs is that the CON team must work with the district to ensure school-level decisions over some staffing choices, to develop district-level plans for computer investment, and to develop district-level plans for a more investment-oriented view of professional development among all district schools. It thus finds itself beginning to evolve into a comprehensive design.

In like manner, the RW design worked with the State of Maryland and St. Mary's County to help pilot an integrated social service network to support the schools. It now has a much fuller vision of what a strong system of support for children could be—including fundamental changes to the delivery of social services, more ambitious than its family support coordinator role. It has formally incorporated this into its design as "something to work for" when conditions of support are auspicious. Meanwhile, the CON school in Worcester, Massachusetts, has begun to work more closely with social service agencies to serve student needs in this regard. This is less the case for the AC or EL schools.

The main difference still remaining between the core designs and comprehensive designs is that the core design teams do not enter into negotiations with sites with models of new governance, staffing, or integrated social services to be adopted or adapted. Instead, they tend to talk of these as barriers to be overcome, whereas the comprehensive and systemic design talk of these as elements of designs. Core designs see governance and staffing as changes in the system necessary to make their designs permanent, as opposed to being elements of their designs, i.e., they don't care how its done so long as it is done. The comprehensive designs tend to demand that firmer and specific models of governance, social services, or staffing be developed over time and include these as parts of their designs.

What seems clear from all this is that whether the issues of governance, staffing, and social services are treated as a starting point in the design or as a bridge to cross when necessary, all design teams had to face issues concerning these elements as they tried to move from initiation to institutionalization of the design. Each team has developed approaches to dealing with these issues; some are direct, others more opportunistic.

Given the general inability of the comprehensive and systemic teams to produce implementation levels as high as some of the core design teams, we think the findings indicate that a more well-thought-out phasing approach might have produced stronger results. NASDC's goal of implementation of all elements within the Phase 2 time period might have prevented this problem. In the end, all designs aim to make certain changes eventually in governance, staffing, and social services, and a phasing approach might help accomplish this.

Changes in Approaches to Design Development

The teams, as they finished Phase 2, began to change their approaches to design development. Some of the details of this will be more apparent in the next chapter on implementation strategies. CON, EL, LALC, and MRSH had intended from the beginning that their designs become less dependent on site development over time as the team benefited from materials and models or curriculum developed by sites in Phase 2. As the Phase 2 sites develop more materials and try out different combinations of student assignment or instructional strategies, these teams intend to cull the lessons and provide firmer models to future sites. Importantly, CON, EL, and MRSH still believe that a significant amount of curriculum must be developed by teachers at new sites so that teachers can go through the process of learning how to use standards, curriculum, instruction, assessments, and student assignments in a coherent way. These teams believe that the value to teachers of learning how to fit these pieces together by doing it themselves far outweighs the value of a neat and orderly curriculum package delivered to a school. However, new schools will benefit from lessons learned and from models, materials, and examples of excellent units developed in Phase 2. Thus, some of the turmoil of Phase 2 in regard to site-based development and issues raised as to site capability might be reduced.

This will not be the case for AT, CLC, or NA. Site capability for development will still persist as an issue, because the teams intend to assist in a fundamentally school-level development process of learning and growth. However, even at this extreme, the process developed for doing this during Phase 2 promises to be more streamlined now that the design is more firmly developed.

Changes to the Sequence of Implementation

A final development was that several teams had learned more about which elements to introduce first and which to implement later—again indicative of a phasing strategy that was not easily accomplished in the NASDC Phase 2 regime. A general consensus, with the exception of AT and NA, was to move quickly to institute change in curriculum and instruction. For four teams (AC, CON, MRSH, and RW), these curricular and instructional changes would be accompanied by significant changes in student assignments within the schools and within the classroom. AT, CLC, MRSH, and NA would focus on setting up the internal governance structure and school improvement planning process as fundamental in bringing about other changes, but they would not force school-level autonomy, staffing changes, or integrated social services. These elements would be fixed goals that would unfold in an opportunistic manner geared to site-level conditions. None of the teams is still pushing toward implementation of all elements simultaneously.

IMPLICATIONS FOR PHASE 3 AND REFORM

Our analysis indicated that team readiness, the number of sites, the type of design, and the approach to demonstration in Phase 2 had strong effects on progress in Phase 2. Some of these differences in progress, however, have less to do with the quality of the efforts of teams and more to do with the types of changes they attempted in the period of time provided. Thus, at least some part of the relative progress is an artifact of the NASDC goals of implementing all elements within a two-year period. All teams, whether core, comprehensive, or systemic, agree that some changes take far longer than the time period allowed by NASDC. The evidence also indicates that NASDC's push toward full implementation, although it encouraged diligent effort, might have prevented more useful phasing strategies from being fully developed.

Team readiness was key in producing progress during Phase 2; however, it is likely to manifest itself in Phase 3 in a different manner. The very purpose of the demonstration phase was to permit the working out of solutions to organizational development problems and to develop the designs to a point where they were well documented and well tested. The challenge was to assemble the talents and skills of members to develop the design and implement it in a few schools, usually in an environment that was relatively well funded. The dropping of LALC from the initial stages of Phase 3, the reorganization of AT, and the spring 1995 progress of EL indicate that the more severe issues concerned with lack of a well-specified design might have been reduced.

The team readiness challenge in Phase 3 will be for all teams to build their capacity to serve more sites. The experiences of NA, with its many sites, indicate the possible difficulties that will be faced in Phase 3 as teams strive to develop the capacity to serve more sites. NA had difficulty beginning with a large number of sites. On the other hand, some of the teams have shown the capability to grow to more sites, even as they were developing design capacity. There is some indication that the design teams can grow over time to serve more sites.[12]

---

[12]Other reform organizations have rapidly increased the number of sites in which they work. For example, Henry Levin's Accelerated Schools began at two pilot sites in

Significant differences between the goals of core, comprehensive, and systemic designs will remain during Phase 3 but have diminished from the stark differences evident at the beginning of Phase 2. Although core design teams have begun, of necessity, to take on some school and district governance issues and staffing concerns because of systemic barriers to their designs, they do not require these as part of the design. Rather, these issues are addressed over time as the design implementation brings them to the fore. Core designs do not usually require blanket changes of district policy, but some school-level autonomy over specific decisions is needed. The very significant and ambitious changes in governance, staffing, and social services desired by the comprehensive and systemic designs always promise to take a long time and might be beyond the capability of most teams without a predisposed jurisdiction and community. Thus, comprehensive and systemic designs will always take longer to implement their vision, and their success will be more susceptible to site capability than will core designs.

Significant differences will continue to exist between designs in the demands they make upon schools for time and resources, especially in the area of curriculum development. This should be understood by new sites entering into agreements with teams. Importantly for reform in general, no firm agreement exists as to a best approach to getting teachers to use new curriculum or how to develop it. The NASDC teams took different approaches and, at least from Phase 2 evidence, several contrasting ones appear to have been useful. Whether teachers develop the curriculum or a team does appears to be less important than that in both cases the teacher's burden is reduced by the provision of standards, curriculum frameworks, and solid materials for development (McLaughlin, 1990).

The findings indicate that, all else equal, schools cannot muster the capacity to enact the many reforms advanced by teams within the limited period of time provided and to the extent demanded by NASDC's goals. The more reformers rely on teachers to specify, de-

---

1987–1988. By 1990, they were in 54 sites and by 1994–1995 they were in over 700 sites. This required the development of regional centers in fall 1990. The Coalition of Essential Schools under Ted Sizer started with 10 schools in 1984–1985. When they linked to Re:Learning in 1988 they had grown to 99. In 1993–1994 they had grown to over 820 schools.

velop, and implement the reforms, the more this is the case. Attempting major changes across many elements is draining on teachers. Thus, teams with ambitious designs might be forced into slower progress as they are limited by teacher time and the capacity of teachers to absorb multiple changes at once. As the number of elements grows and the number of sites grows, the teams will be increasingly challenged to develop new and more extensive competencies in many areas of reform, implying the need for further support of the teams over time as they ripen and mature.

Chapter Five

ASSISTANCE STRATEGIES AND THEIR EFFECT ON PROGRESS

This chapter explores more specifically *how* the design teams inter-acted with sites as agents of change. It is divided into two parts. The first deals with the selection process of sites. The second explores how different ways of interaction and different implementation strategies in schools affected the progress of teams and the lessons teams drew from those experiences. The implications are drawn at the close of the chapter. This chapter should put the preceding one in further perspective. It was not enough for a team to have a well-crafted design. A strong implementation strategy that matched the design was equally important to successfully meeting NASDC's goals for Phase 2.

ACHIEVING INITIAL COMMITMENT FROM SITES IN THE SELECTION PROCESS

The selection of sites and initial interactions should help to ensure that the school understands the design vision and is committed to it from the beginning. This initial commitment ensures that schools have not been coerced into a change program and thus are unlikely to undermine the effort through strong resistance. Our findings re-garding the process used and the results indicate that in many cases schools did not make a well-informed choice and firm commitment to the design was not gained in the initial selection process.

The published baseline report on the fall 1993 site visits for this study described the initial site selection process for Phase 2 We found the following:

- Several teams chose potential sites based on previous personal contacts between the districts, schools, and teams, often with the district choosing the site rather than the design team (AC, CON, AT, NA, and RW). This was due to the hurried nature of initiation imposed by NASDC deadlines. Some did try to institute a more formal application process with deliberate selection, but they were not consistently successful (EL, CLC, LALC, and MRSH).

- Most teams intended to ensure early teacher commitment in the selection process by encouraging majority votes and also encouraging teachers not interested in the design to transfer to another school. But these ideas were applied irregularly across sites within teams.

- Sites selected designs looking for gain, not recognizing the effort needed to reform. Sites reported that they chose to work with design teams because they wanted additional resources, especially new technology; access to professional development and/or the legitimacy gained from association with reputable reformers; and the design (as they understood it), because it matched where they were headed. The idea that there would be multiple reasons for adoption of a design or a reform is discussed in Huberman and Miles (1984). Principals and teachers did not talk of the resources they would have to expend or the work they would have to do.

- Because some designs were not fully developed, there was some confusion on the part of principals and school staff about what they were selecting. Thus, the decision to become a Phase 2 site was often made on faith, not on firm information.

- Several design teams indicated that some sites were chosen because of the perceived ability to succeed in implementing NASDC designs. The sites were believed to have implemented parts of the design already and therefore would show early successful implementation. (Note that our assessment criteria discount this approach. We assign progress only when the team itself produces the change in the school.)

All teams reported poor initial commitment in at least some of their sites. The lack of a true commitment to a design or poor selection process manifested themselves in different ways, for example:

- In interviews at more than one site associated with each team, teachers told us that they did approve the design after the principal framed the question as, "agree to do this and get discretionary funds or don't agree and get no discretionary funds." When implementation began, the teachers had committed not to the design, only to the receipt of resources, and they resented the demands made upon them.

- The principal volunteered the school for participation without full support of the staff. The staff continued to express anger over the top-down decision well into implementation and a core group of staff refused to implement the design or lagged in doing so. Huberman and Miles (1984, p. 40) cite an example of how teachers often chose to adopt reform: "the principal wanted it; we got the message." This was very similar to what we heard at the majority of sites that took formal votes.

- For teams that gave significant amounts of funding to the schools to participate, some schools voiced little initial commitment to many of the design elements. The schools purchased computer equipment and recommended materials and used professional development days, but they did not commit to the principles of the design or wanted to pick and choose among elements to implement.

- For those teams that were still specifying and developing their designs as they entered schools, initial interactions were confused. The less developed the design, the more initial confusion at the sites in terms of what staff were supposed to do. Sites simply reflected the confusion of some of the teams.

- Some jurisdictions had policies that would prevent the implementation of the design and the design teams did not know about these at the selection time.

Some part of the variation in progress among design teams must be due to this poor selection process, though an absolute correlation is not possible. As the remainder of this discussion will indicate, poor initial commitment can be overcome with effort.

REVISION OF SELECTION STRATEGIES

In the final set of interviews with design teams and sites, we asked "what worked well to promote the required changes in the school and what did not work well?" When specifically addressing the selection and initial commitment process, the consensus was clear:

1. Obviously, a more fully developed design, documented in easily readable form, would be helpful.

2. Teams and sites agreed that the team should present the design to the whole school. Both agree that this would help avoid problems of misinterpretation that plagued several teams and schools, "selling" by principals, or assignment by districts.

3. Teachers should be involved in the decision to accept a design. Some teams now require a formal, anonymous vote by teachers. For example, AC and RW require an 80 percent vote and transfer of teachers who are not willing to implement. Others are less specific, not requiring a formal vote, but requiring a "getting-to-know-you period" where teachers are introduced to the design and debate undertaking it (for example, AT).

4. In making a choice, the design teams preferred that schools actually enter into a search for a design suitable to their needs.[1]

REQUIRED INTERACTIONS AND SUPPORTS FOR REFORMING SCHOOLS

In focus groups at the sites, we asked teachers and administrators what interactions and supports they thought they needed to undertake their design tasks. The results of the group interviews were straightforward. Our findings indicate that principals and teachers

---

[1]In fact, introduction to sites in Phase 3 calls for a "design team fair" in each of several jurisdictions where schools can "shop" among the designs. Formal votes by staff are called for and the design teams have developed much more elaborate information packets than existed in Phase 2 selection.

were fairly consistent across all sites in what they felt was needed to promote change, regardless of the particular design. Our findings, which indicate that the following elements would be part of a well received implementation strategy, echo findings of Fullan (1991), Gitlin and Margonis (1995), Herman and Stringfield (1995), Muncey (1994), Muncey and McQuillian (1993), Prestine and Bowen (1993), and Rosenholtz (1989).

- An introduction to the design by the team that was compelling— or at least clear—and that was provided to *all* administrators and staff.

- Relevant training provided to *all* administrators and teachers at the school with behavioral changes or new processes modeled.

- Concrete materials to use in classrooms, committees, or other fo- rums for reform.

- Presence of the design team members to help staff and/or pres- ence of a facilitator to help their understanding on a day-to-day basis.

- Teacher teaming to work on design issues or curriculum devel- opment.

- Participatory governance to ensure continued teacher support of the design.

- Teacher time for curriculum development, teacher-to-teacher interactions, and becoming adept at new behaviors (time for practice at the individual and school level).

- Exposure to new ideas.

- Resources to support the functions mentioned above.

Teachers and design teams did indicate that these components of a implementation strategy can substitute for each other. For example, strong documentation of a design can substitute at least somewhat for training and facilitators at the site. In addition, some imple- mentation components might be more important for some types of designs. Teacher time was significantly more important for sites working to develop their own curriculum with a design team that used a site-based development approach than it was for a team that supplied curriculum units.

Implementation Components Associated with Design Teams

Initial content analysis of the design documents in fall 1993 indicated a disturbing lack of attention in the proposals to implementation strategies. Much more attention was paid to the design itself. Content analysis gave little indication that the teams had given much thought to how to get a design into a school, aside from the large distinction between the team development approach and the site development approaches and the distinction between teams using a lead teacher model.

During each site visit, we asked staff from each school, "What types of support did you receive from the team to implement the design and was it useful? " The results of the teachers' and administrators feedback on what they received from design teams, compared to what they said was needed, is presented in Figure 5.1.[2]

We found that design teams differed dramatically in their interactions with the sites (after selection and initial voting) and their role or their associated school's ability to provide the support teachers and administrators indicated was helpful. The following sums up the implications when added to material already covered in Chapter Three concerning progress the teams made toward NASDC goals.

- AC and RW, teams that we indicated made substantial progress toward their goals, were also associated in teachers' and administrators' minds with having many components of a strong implementation strategy.

- CON, CLC, and MRSH used strong strategies, improved them over time, and made moderate to substantial progress on elements.

---

[2]The strong consensus among the teachers we spoke with lead us to suspect that a survey using similar questions would reproduce our results with high reliability. We note that further support of these findings is indicated by the reactions of the design teams. AT, LALC, and NA admit that their implementation strategies have not produced the results they desired and are in the process of restructuring them.

- Teachers and administrators indicated that the EL strategy was very strong for getting under way, but that it did not provide longer-term aid in all areas. This team was associated with lower levels of progress by the end of Phase 2.

- Teachers and administrators indicated that LALC, AT, and NA did not give them the needed assistance in the first year, but these teams improved by the second. Teachers associated this slow progress with poor implementation strategies.

Introduction to All Staff

Teachers and administrators valued heavily a team's ability to present the design concepts in a coherent fashion to *all* teachers and administrators after the initial decision to proceed.

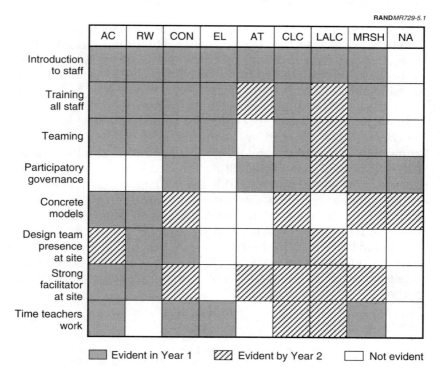

Figure 5.1—Implementation Strategies by Design

They believed that a strong introduction provided to all staff acted to guide all members, bringing everyone on board.

For at least two reasons, this did not happen with some designs. First, some designs were not fully developed when introduced into the schools. Thus, the description of the design was less than compelling and more likely to be confused. Second, in some cases the design was introduced to only a small portion of the staff, with the expectation that these staff would spread the word to others. What often happened instead was that this approach created an "in group" of staff and an "out group," immediately setting up conflicts.

AC and RW were the most developed designs at the point when the introductory sessions were made. In addition, both teams made efforts to have all staff attend introductory sessions. Other teams also had strong beginnings in this regard, such as EL and MRSH.

Three teams (AT, LALC, and NA) using lead-teacher approaches where only a few teachers were introduced to the design and without fully specified designs (because of dependence on local specification or because the team had not specified the design at that point) faced considerable obstacles in the first year in getting all teachers to know what the design was and to support it.[3] Interviews with teachers at schools associated with these designs indicated that a handful of teachers—those involved in the introductory training—had strong knowledge of the design and its key features, whereas other teachers frankly admitted that they had little knowledge of the design or were unsure. Those less knowledgeable did not know what the new goals of the school were or how they were to pursue those goals differently from before. All teachers attributed this state of affairs to the model of introduction used. When asked at the end of Phase 2 how the process could have been improved they indicated that the design should have been introduced to the whole staff from the very beginning as one teacher put it, "to get us all going on the same page, working together. "

---

[3]Past research on the Coalition of Essential Schools has identified this "train-the-trainer" model as producing "jealousies" and factions within the staff. See Muncey and McQuillian (1993), Muncey (1994), and Herman and Stringfield (1995).

AT, LALC, and NA became aware of this issue during the first year of Phase 2 and began measures to deal with it including more extensive training for more people. But the selective introduction had already slowed down efforts and lapsed progress could not be made up quickly with these complex designs.

Training for All Staff

Teachers and administrators indicated that training should include discussions of the reasons for change, the theory behind it, and hands-on practice as much as possible. Respondents said the latter was especially important when significantly new behaviors were desired. They also felt it was important to reinforce behaviors through feedback during training sessions and in coaching and other supports at the job site. As with the introduction to the design, respondents felt the training should be widespread—available to all staff, not just a few. Teachers leveled strong criticisms at teams that provided training to only a narrow set of teachers (such as the AT, LALC, and NA teams, which use lead-teacher or train-the-trainer models).

Training was provided by all teams. School personnel, by and large, valued most training experiences. The value placed on the training varied according to certain factors. School personnel appeared to value:

- Sessions that introduced the general concept of the design and its elements and provided them with a purpose and a framework for placing priority on certain activities.

- Concentrated time spent on a specific element or component of an element and the change desired. In this type of session, they valued immediate follow-up on questions or problems, the chance to observe others demonstrate desired behaviors, and hands-on participation in activities.

- Attending training together as teams or having the opportunity to work with other teachers who had students with similar characteristics or who were from similar districts.

Some design teams appear to offer unique experiences that helped school personnel understand the nature of the design. For these teams, most teachers thought the sessions were very useful. Some examples follow. Their common theme is teachers working together in teams on real problems.

AC does not provide for very much training compared with the other teams—only five days during the summer immediately before the beginning of the school year. However, all teachers and administrators attend this training together and it is very intensive. Because the design is largely specified and models and materials are already developed, training can immediately focus on concrete changes to be made. Furthermore, teachers reported that the AC vision provides clear priorities for them, which allows them to focus their efforts.

Each summer, CLC provided for teams of teachers from its sites to meet together for a prolonged time to hear speakers and work on issues of concern to the school. School personnel report that these have been highly valuable sessions because the agenda is largely set by the school and the school teams work out the issues then and there with the facilitation of the CLC teams and other experts.

EL provided for selected teams of teachers to go on an Outward Bound expedition in the summer before beginning implementation. Teachers consistently reported that the opportunity for working in their teacher teams, in unusual and challenging circumstances, provided a "jolt" that allowed them to experience several concepts inherent to the vision of the design: Everyone can learn, everyone has unique talents that can be brought to bear on formidable problems, and everyone can accomplish new and different things, but only when working in groups can major challenges be overcome. The learning of teachers occurred through actual experience, not formal instruction, thus emphasizing the project-based, activity-driven nature of instruction that EL wished to promote.

The format of the training offered was important to school personnel, but teachers also emphasized the need for training in many areas—some areas not usually thought to be needed. For example, because many teams tried to institute school governance committees, committee members appreciated training in budgeting, scheduling, and team dynamics. Several teams (AC, CLC, CON, LALC, NA, and RW) wanted teachers to become more adept at outreach in the community. Teachers stated that they needed some help in understanding how to present themselves to businesses and parents in ways that would encourage those groups to volunteer time, resources, etc.

All teams and school administrators agreed that in the first year they did not provide enough training for principals or other school administrators. Rather, most teams focused almost exclusively on teachers.[4] By the end of the first year of Phase 2, principals or teachers at several schools had complained directly to their design teams about the need for principal training. This seemed to be especially the case for design teams calling for changes to school governance, which would naturally affect principals and their roles (AT, LALC, MRSH, and NA). By the second year of Phase 2 more teams were developing training courses specifically designed for the administrators. As team leaders from LALC and MRSH indicated, this oversight crucially delayed their progress at sites. Plans by LALC and MRSH and several other teams (AT, CON, and NA) now specifically include early training of administrators in participatory governance.

Teaming and Participatory Governance

Each design team incorporated the use of teacher teams into its implementation strategy and at most sites teaming by teachers for purposes connected to the design increased over the two-year period.

- Six (AC, CON, EL, CLC, LALC, and MRSH) used teacher teams for curriculum development.

- Six (CON, CLC, EL, LALC, MRSH, and RW) used teacher teams because of a move to multi-year, multi-age, or other student groupings, which required teachers to act in teams to oversee a group of students.

- Seven teams (AT, CON, CLC, LALC, MRSH, NA, and RW) included teachers on participatory governance committees. (In the case of RW this was in keeping with the Maryland state

---

[4]When asked why this oversight occurred, most teams simply indicated they had focused almost exclusively on teachers as the focus of change. They now recognize the importance of involving the entire school.

mandate for site-based management rather than with an element of the design.) In implementation this often meant that each teacher was assigned to one of several teams in the school working on design-related issues.

- Several schools adopted community health teams, which promote interactions among teachers and specialists.

The manner in which teacher participation in teams was ensured varied by school as well as team. Because of this, we heard varying views about the efficacy of the teams. For example, in schools where teachers were required to participate or were assigned to a committee, teachers less interested in the activity complained about the teaming.

Discounting this effect, we found that most teachers by the end of Phase 2 indicated that teaming was essential to the design and they did not want to give it up. Some noted that it could be significantly reduced, but they still thought it produced important benefits. These benefits depended on the type of team and whether it had worked productively.[5] Important benefits mentioned include:

- Reduction in the isolation of teachers and growing excitement about their jobs, as teachers began to share information, ideas, and problems with each other. Teachers at every school indicated that this proved to be a fundamental turning point in their careers. Having been burnt-out and lonely before the teaming, for the first time in many years they felt connected to their peers and focused on improvement.

- The building of a culture of reflective practice as teachers began to discuss problems and potential solutions with peers and build common agreement on effective approaches to educational issues or design problems worked out through teams or committees. Again, teachers at each school indicated that they believed their performance had improved because now they were responsible to their peers and could no longer hide poor practices.

---

[5]As Kruse and Louis (1995) did, we found that teams could be very detrimental to schoolwide efforts when the ill effects associated with isolation of teachers becomes associated with isolated teams. Thus, teaming is not a universal solution but one that must be managed well to have the effects desired.

- Work produced such as developed units with the benefit of more "brain power" or thought put into each unit because of the team effort.

- Higher levels of commitment to the design associated with serving on participatory governance committees or just having some teachers with a voice in what was once a top-down system. This latter statement was made with some astonishment by teachers who on reflection said that their participation meant that they could no longer wait for the "latest of many reforms they had been told to do" to go away. They were part of the process of decisionmaking and could no longer avoid responsibility.

Concrete Models and Materials

Teachers talked in general of the need for concrete materials. By this, they meant both models for new behaviors and specific materials to be used in classrooms.

A model is an example for imitation or a pattern for something to be constructed by the administrators and teachers. Models can describe newly desired behaviors, for example, offering specific descriptions of how to deliver instruction in a project-based classroom. They can be descriptors, offering steps in the process of creating, and examples of how to create, interdisciplinary units that are standards-based. Clear models are ones that school-level personnel can read, view, or otherwise expose themselves to so they understand specifically how their tasks must change. Models could be provided for many different parts of a design: a model of how to function in a team decisionmaking process, detailed examples of scope and sequences in schools adopting the design, detailed examples of new scheduling options to promote the design, descriptions of appropriate grades for multi-age groupings, or a video of how to teach in such situations, with examples of portfolios with rubrics and how to use them.

Without these specific models, school personnel said they did not have strong understandings upon which to change their behaviors; and several teams did not provide the models needed. Some of this is attributable to the low level of development of certain elements at the time of our initial visits. In several cases, schools were implementing before the design team had developed models. However, these complaints were not common to all teams. Rather, teachers associated with teams using a site-based development approach were more likely to voice this problem. Why?

Several teams relying heavily on a site-based development approach initially thought that the provision of concrete models would deprive teachers of their input, which the teams felt was needed to ensure continuing commitment, or would deprive them of the chance to construct their own curriculum to ensure in-depth understanding. CON, EL, AT, CLC, LALC, MRSH, and NA teams wanted teachers to develop their own curriculum because the teams believed that this would create teacher buy-in. The argument went that teachers creating their own curriculum would certainly want to use it and would not feel that higher authorities had imposed ideas upon them. By relying on site development, these teams sought to create more permanent change. In addition, AT, CLC, and EL all held philosophically to constructivist views that urged student-centered development (i.e., students and teachers working jointly to develop shared understanding) to promote deeper understandings and truly changed behavior patterns. Fearful of appearing too prescriptive, these teams initially provided teachers with rather vague ideas about curricular goals. They did not provide frameworks or concrete examples of a strong curriculum. Several did not have standards statements (EL, CLC, AT, and NA).

Teachers in this situation complained that they did not have concrete models upon which to develop new curriculum. Left largely to their own devices, teachers reported they did whatever they were already best at doing. In the first year of Phase 2, sites associated with these teams made very slow and very inconsistent curriculum development efforts. The teams now are developing quality-control mechanisms for the curriculum units developed and more concrete models to guide further efforts.

In contrast, those schools guided by strong, standards-based models, such as AC, MRSH, and RW, voiced few complaints about the curriculum or very specific ones and made strong progress on implementing the curriculum. The fact that the complaints were so specific—a particular unit was not good enough or a standard had not been covered—we took to be a sign of strong implementation, in that the teachers had become knowledgeable about the models and could critique them. AC and RW provided for teacher feedback to improve the curriculum, and this feedback has materially affected subsequent development.

This theme has appeared in several elements besides curriculum. Teachers associated with CON, EL, and MRSH asked for specific models of multi-age grouping, modeling of teaching techniques for those groupings, and examples of "good" versus "bad" portfolios. Committees associated with AT asked for comparative models of new standards so that they could usefully deliberate upon alternatives. Those associated with NA asked for better descriptors of "high performance management" and "community services integration."

Thus, there appears to be a balance required between overprescribing behaviors in models, thus encouraging resistance or shallow change, or underdefining behaviors through a lack of models and encouraging confusion. Properly understood and used, concrete models do not dictate behaviors but pave the way for better understanding and purposeful effort toward reform on the part of teachers.[6] Addressing this balance and teachers' almost ingrained expectations for easy answers appears to be a major challenge for the designs that subscribe to constructivism.

Teachers also used the term "concrete materials" to indicate design team provision of materials to aid school personnel in the classroom including curriculum units and lesson plans, textbooks, materials for use in projects, tests, and assessments.

Design teams and teachers reported that there was a dearth of age-appropriate materials for project-based learning. For example, the AC curriculum framework requires that second-grade students explore and create a constructive action on the theme "We use government to improve our community." However, few publishing companies produce materials on government for second-graders. Thus, teachers had to search for their own or develop their own. This took additional time and placed a burden on second-grade teachers. Other examples are more general. Teachers stated that they could not find interdisciplinary, project-based curriculum materials for the

---

[6]This finding is supported by McLaughlin (1990).

lower grade levels. Such material was simply not available. Thus, they spent considerable time searching for any snippets that were available or spent time developing it themselves.

This has driven several teams to push more strongly for the sharing of curriculum units and materials across sites to reduce the development effort of teachers. Several teams have now introduced computer-based networks, or other means for the sharing of curriculum units. These are new and have yet to reach their full potential.

Teams have developed materials throughout Phase 2 and during summer 1995, including descriptions of the design elements and resource guidebooks for those elements, and will in the future find better ways to share materials among sites. Thus, much of the confusion we saw in Phase 2 schools should be reduced. By Phase 3, the teams might enter sites with more of the materials and models required by teachers.

Design Team Presence and Facilitators at the Site

Teachers and administrators highly valued, when provided, both regular face-to-face interactions with design team members and the use of facilitators from the school who coached or helped them understand, practice, and implement the design. Teachers who did not have these two supports, or had only one, indicated that these types of supports were needed for more progress to be made.

Design Team Presence. Design team presence was valued by school personnel. The greater the number and regularity of visits of design team members in the school, the fewer complaints we heard and the greater the ability of personnel to talk knowledgeably about the design and its elements. School personnel associated with design teams that did not visit sites complained that they did not understand the design, their design team was not providing enough feedback, or the team did not know enough about the school to understand the difficulties of reform. Substitutes for design team members, such as school-level facilitators, only partially filled this need. Our understanding from focus groups is that one part of the need appears to be associated with school personnel having confidence that the team members understood site needs. We note that those teams working with many sites or with sites that are not located nearby have greater difficulty fulfilling this need, implying that geographic proximity and resources are important factors in helping transform schools.

Site Facilitators. Several teams used school-level facilitators as a way to increase the development and demonstration of designs in the school (AC, CON, LALC, and RW). In the AC and RW models, the facilitator is chosen from the school staff and in most cases is paid for with school funds; CON hires its own facilitator from outside the school staff. In all three cases, all the teachers receive significant training of their own; thus, the facilitator did not act in a "train-the-trainer" mode or as a lead teacher. CLC added a site facilitator in the second year.

The reaction of the AC and RW teachers to this arrangement has been positive. The facilitators receive additional training in the design and in observation. Their purpose is to help teachers on an individual basis with implementing the design. They are constantly available to other teachers for questions, to address immediate concerns, and to model teaching practices in the classroom. Thus, they function to provide a permanent and readily available resource for the teachers when questions about the design or its implementation arise. Colleagues of these facilitators did not voice jealousy or talk about special privileges; rather, they indicated that these facilitators were highly respected and had very difficult jobs.

The LALC team used a facilitator in a different circumstance. The LALC design calls for participatory management, but the team had difficulty getting administrators and teachers to work collectively together. It created the position of a "change agent" to work with the school staff toward more participatory governance. This facilitator sat in on meetings and helped bring out points of contention in a neutral way to show how the manner in which decisions were being made was affecting the decision. Administrators and teachers credit this strategy with enabling them to make considerable progress in schools previously ridden with labor-management strife.

On the other hand, school staff not associated with these designs indicated that such a position would have been useful. They talked of the difficulties of long-distance communication with teams and the need to have some on-site experts who could help them through the process of applying the techniques learned at workshops to their classrooms.

Teacher Time for Reform

The teams and sites differed in their ability to provide time to school-level personnel for development and demonstration. Time had several different dimensions as used by teachers: noninstructional time during the school year to read and understand models, develop curriculum, and work jointly on new elements; noninstructional time for training; and time to assimilate and become proficient in the new behaviors at an individual, team, and school level.

Regardless of the time provided, across all teams and all sites school-level staff pleaded for more noninstructional time within a school year and for more years to implement reform before results were judged. In the words of many, "change was taking place too fast" or "was taking place in so many areas we will never get it all done." This was especially an issue for those schools associated with teams that required significant teacher development of curriculum or other elements.

Several barriers stood in the way of many schools in creating the time needed. But teams and schools often found ways to cope.

Some districts simply did not have the funding needed to provide additional staff development days for training associated with the design. Partly this was a function of a constrained budget in districts on the verge of bankruptcy. However, in many cases it came from an inability or unwillingness of districts to favor some schools over others by providing discretionary funds to a few selected schools. School-level respondents tended to call this "politics as usual."

Some design teams took early action to avoid this problem, most notably CLC, which chose to work with schools only after reaching agreement with the district that the school would have up to 20 days of staff development time per teacher. Some of this was paid for by CLC, but much of it was paid for by the districts. Other teams, including AT, CON, EL, and MRSH, overcame budget constraints by providing their own funds for this activity.

By rearranging the schedule, schools created blocks of noninstructional time for teachers and provided for common planning time. This was especially useful for site-developed schools in which teachers needed to work in groups to develop interdisciplinary curriculum. The ability to rearrange the schedule or the inclination to do so appeared to vary by school and not team. Some schools associated with each team chose to do so, others associated with the same team did not.

In most cases at the elementary level, the provision of block noninstructional time was possible through the use of "special" teachers in music, physical education, art, and health. These teachers could hold joint classes while regular classroom teachers met as a group. Several issues arose regarding this use of "special" time. First, districts often programmed special teachers' schedules before all others because they go from school to school. Without cooperation from the district and the special teachers as to scheduling, the school was unable to manipulate the schedule to provide block time. Second, this precluded special teachers from taking part in any work on interdisciplinary curriculum during those times.

For those teams relying on teachers for significant development of the curriculum or other parts of the design, the inability to gain some noninstructional time for teachers during the school year remained a strong constraint on progress. Teachers could not produce curriculum without being given time to do so. Thus, the implementation of some elements of these designs was heavily dependent on the ability of teams and districts to cooperate and come up with funds or new schedules to provide for time. This lack of time was strongly related in teachers' minds with the inability to move from pilots (beginning implementation) to fuller school implementation (moderate to substantial implementation). The schedule and lack of professional development days, as they saw it, did not allow all teachers to participate fully in the reform effort. This was almost universally expressed as "asking us to change the wheel of the car while moving at sixty miles per hour."

In this regard, teachers often noted that they need both blocks of time, say a week or two in the summer, as well as routine time during the school year for this type of activity. Much work can be accomplished in the summer, but refinements and improvements take place during the school year as the curriculum is experienced by real students.

The designs teams, while scrambling to provide teacher time, indicated that some of the time provided was not put to good use, in part because of lack of materials to guide activities. Several teams voiced less concern about providing more time and more concern about ensuring that time provided was effectively used. Teams associated with less well developed designs hoped that better formats and clearer instructions and their learning would increase the effective use of time.

Design teams and site personnel argued that a good percentage of the time needed is peculiar to transition and is not a permanent characteristic of the school. Teams that relied on site-based development in Phase 2 might be able to reduce time requirements in Phase 3 as they develop transferable materials, models, and curriculum units from Phase 2 sites.

However, no one argued that the total time to transform a school could be significantly reduced by increasing the amount of noninstructional time during the school year. Although some relationship between the two concepts of time exists, they are not directly substitutable. Respondents appear to believe that some amount of practice over several years with different students and in different situations is necessary to become proficient in a design. This is more so for designs such as AT, CLC, and EL, which place strong emphasis on constructivism, student-centered learning, and site-based development.

RELATIONSHIP BETWEEN IMPLEMENTATION AND RESOURCES

The strategies and mechanisms that appear to be particularly effective in infusing the designs into the schools depend on some source of additional funding at least during the transformation phase. Professional development, release time or noninstructional time, materials, computers and computer networks, and facilitators all require funding at the site. Often, this funding was supplemented by grants, district funds, etc., making it difficult to determine the total funding package and its relationship to effects. This was further complicated by the fact that the need for funding to implement a design varied as much by school as by design. This issue will be covered in more detail in forthcoming work by Ross.

IMPLICATIONS

Findings indicate that, along with factors such as design type, team readiness, number of sites, and design approach, the differences in implementation strategy among teams help explain the variance in teams' immediate progress toward NASDC goals.

Our findings indicate that which combination of implementation components a team used was less important than the mix of components that supported the particular design. Although the staff at sites made it clear that the implementation strategy was as important as the design, they also made it clear that the strategy was not formulaic. Rather, the sites and teams working together during development had to match design and implementation to effectively produce change. Some appeared to be more successful than others.

Our findings also indicate that teachers and administrators cannot operate effectively to change their behaviors without concrete supports offered to all parties, such as materials, models, facilitators, teaming, and noninstructional time. These supports require funding at the school level.

In addition, the experiences of the schools we sampled indicated that initial commitment to a design was not always achieved and could be fleeting without long-term support. Long-term commitment by teachers is developed over time in a working relationship where a team and a school staff interact with each other toward common goals. Commitment comes when teachers are supported and begin to see the results of their efforts. Beautiful-sounding ideas or visions do not engender the day-to-day work needed to transform a school. Strong assistance in understanding what needs to be changed, concrete models, coaching, and time produced change and therefore more commitment. It is the ever spiraling process of discovery and recommitment that transform a school (McLaughlin, 1990).

The findings also support the contention that the types of whole-school reforms supported by NASDC take longer to implement than the two-year period provided. Some teams can make rapid progress on certain elements, but teachers and administrators at all sites expressed the need for more time to institutionalize the designs. Those teams dedicated to site development of curriculum, for strong philosophical and well as practical implementation reasons, might always be expected to take longer to produce observable implementation. Increasing the release or noninstructional time for teachers might remove some limits on progress, but it is unlikely to substitute for a continuum of time over which to become adept at design practices.

In short, it is still not clear whether the different implementation approaches eventually produce improved student outcomes. We are reporting only on observable changes in a short period of time and statements by teachers about the process. Several design teams have noted that the constructivist views they have advocated necessarily take longer to implement and that initial teachers' complaints are due to the false expectations for rapid improvement and change built up by failed or disreputable past approaches.

Furthermore, more complex designs, with more elements that involve changes to the external bureaucratic structure or that require significant teacher development of elements, will take more time, even as the teams become more adept at assistance. Thus, the NASDC whole-school effort should not be judged by the standards dictated by past efforts at limited programmatic changes in schools.

Clearly, by the end of Phase 2 teams had moved to provide better support for teachers, and the further definition and documentation of some designs will go a long way toward providing teachers with some of the concrete supports they need. Much of the assistance provided came from design team funding as opposed to internally generated sources. However, Phase 3 will present a more resource-constrained environment to the teams and schools. Thus, teams are now reconstructing their strategies in keeping with the limited resources available to most schools. This might force them into fewer hands-on approaches and more reliance on materials and better-developed designs.

Chapter Six

SYSTEMIC BARRIERS
TO THE INSTITUTIONALIZATION
OF WHOLE-SCHOOL DESIGNS

This chapter addresses some of the systemic barriers to change that manifested themselves in the two-year time frame of Phase 2 and became obstacles to final institutionalization of the designs. It focuses on some of the "cultural changes" that were taking place in schools, or not taking place, as we left them in spring 1995 and the reasons why those changes were or were not occurring. The chapter concentrates on four areas: new definitions of professional development, moves toward school autonomy, clashes between the culture of particular schools and those of the design teams, and the inability of the teams and schools to address issues of public engagement or community involvement.

NEW VISIONS OF PROFESSIONAL DEVELOPMENT IN SCHOOLS

When asked about the contribution of the design team to progress toward student improvement at a site, many teachers and administrators focused on changed professional attitudes now becoming embedded in the school. This was often framed as "working with the design opened our eyes to the possibilities." Possibilities translated into several important concepts, different for different people:

1. The full possibility that all children really could learn challenging content and skills if the teacher committed to this goal and used effective strategies to accomplish it.

2. The possibility that the school and its infrastructure could be re-arranged to enable this to happen.

3. The possibility that teachers could work together to make this happen.

It is our belief that what we saw happening in many schools associated with design teams by the end of Phase 2 was a reconceptualization of "professionalism" in schools, and therefore a reconceptualization of professional development.[1] Schools working with design teams began to accomplish these important changes in attitudes using different approaches to professional development than traditional models adopted for programmatic changes. The traditional model is a one-day workshop or conference to establish a specific programmatic change. More important for significantly changed attitudes from the teacher's point of view, as we have come to understand it, were structural changes to the school and to the teacher's job.

The contribution of the design teams to this sea change, as yet incomplete, was strong. The vision, the practical definition of tasks, the implementation assistance, and the challenge all goaded school staff toward reconceptualizing their jobs and their responsibilities toward each other and the students they serve.

The following discusses some of the mechanisms used to encourage a shift in "belief possibilities," attributed to the design teams by teachers, that contrast with more traditional approaches, which were the norms in the schools before association with design teams. The inability to provide this type of transformative professional development remains a large barrier to whole-school change (Darling-Hammond, 1992).

Challenging Teachers to Take Responsibility

Traditionally, professional development has meant exposing teachers to new ideas and best practices though workshops and training. This was done by all of the NASDC teams and will continue to be

---

[1]Darling-Hammond (1988 and 1992) and Rosenholtz (1989) reflect these ideas about professional development.

done. However, for all of these teams and most of the schools associated with them, professional development has taken on a greater meaning—it encourages the teacher to expand his or her authority and responsibility to the definition of the teaching job itself— including serious consideration of what curriculum, instruction, standards, assessments, and student assignments will be promoted by the school. Professional development is not adopting best practice but taking on the task of defining the job to ensure that goals for students are met.[2]

Teachers credited the teams with challenging them to take responsibility for their own work. By the end of Phase 2, most of the design teams (AC, CON, EL, LALC, MRSH, and RW) had arrived at a point where teachers were asked to review curriculum against a set of standards and begin the process of revision.[3] Three teams (CON, MRSH, and NA) had begun to institute rubrics for judging student work and teachers were working in groups to understand and jointly grade student products using the rubrics. (EL had apparently instituted rubrics at one site not in our sample.) This was most often done in interdisciplinary teams or teams of teachers within a grade level.

Being associated with a design team often meant that teachers no longer could deny their responsibility for the delivery of standards-based curriculum and instruction or allow others to accept responsibility for it. Often for the first time, teachers were taking responsibility for the development of their own curriculum, for ensuring that it met a high standard for both content and skill, and for ensuring that their judgments of student performance met as high a standard as their peers'. This was being accomplished whether the design teams relied on sites for development or whether the team developed most of design.

---

[2]Rosenholtz (1989) hints at this type of activity in her work and how it varies by schools, depending on contextual and social cues that are amenable to manipulation.

[3]The experiences of the other teams were somewhat different. For AT, each school developed its own standards and some teachers in schools were beginning to do this. NA was only just introducing its New Standards in limited areas. CLC initially indicated it would not create standards of its own but would adopt those of Minnesota. The Minnesota standards were overthrown by the state and in year 2, CLC began to develop its own standards.

Teacher Teaming as Professional Development

This challenge to teachers did not happen automatically, and sometimes teachers refused the challenge. But when the teachers took it up, it appeared to be helped by a series of "infrastructure changes" to the schools.

We have already discussed the usefulness of teacher teams for implementation, especially for the development of curriculum. However, teachers pointed out more subtle reasons why teaming became important to the success of the transformation effort.[4]

- Working with teams, especially on governance committees, showed teachers for the first time how traditional scheduling, hiring, firing, and budgeting practices prevented them from incorporating curriculum and instructional reforms into the school. By working together on these teams, they began by the end of Phase 2 to take on these important issues—restructuring the school to support the student goals. In open forums staff discussed the pros and cons of different schedules, attempting to promote a schedule that would most support the tenets of the design. Although evident at many schools, it was most commonly perceived by those schools associated with AC, AT, CLC, CON, LALC, NA, and RW.

- Working with teacher teams across disciplines allowed teachers to understand how over time content standards had squeezed out of the curriculum valuable skills and the ability to apply them. Teacher teams allowed them to understand the larger picture of what a student should have accomplished to graduate. This was further encouraged by standards developed by design teams or newly created by states.

- As mentioned above, teaming decreased the isolation of teachers, opening up the possibility of peer review no matter

---

[4]Rosenholtz (1989) had similar findings. According to her more extensive survey and interviewing, staff noted that teaming was more effective when it was combined with a staff unified around a common strategy or vision. Rosenholtz found that shared school goals had a robust and independent contribution to teacher collaboration. She found that a lack of certainty about teaching or lack of knowledge about what others at the school were doing led to too much self-reliance and little requesting or giving of the information needed to improve practice.

how subtle. At first, teachers avoided criticizing each other, but when teachers were given a standard or a curriculum framework to work with, the peer pressure for performance increased, and teachers report that they began to work to this challenge. This was especially evident in CON and MRSH schools.

Parent, Teacher, and Student Teaming as Professional Development

Five designs (CON, CLC, EL, MRSH, and RW) call for significant interactions between teachers, parents, and students to determine student progress, to set individual goals, and to revise student activities according to progress measured by a portfolio or other type of assessment. This type of teaming also altered the responsibility of teachers and students within the school.

By the end of the second year, schools associated with these teams had moved to multi-age or multi-year grouping or other teacher teams that were responsible for a given student's progress. Working in teams, the teachers reviewed the student's progress and report they were better able to understand an individual student because the student was being seen through multiple eyes and in multiple circumstances.

Teachers, parents, and students we talked with associated with CON, CLC, EL, and MRSH indicated that the involvement of parents and students in a review of the student's progress and construction of an individualized education plan was a powerful tool for increased performance.[5] Parents were given specific and dense information, usually in the form of a portfolio, that allowed them to better understand their child's strengths and weaknesses. Parents and teachers report becoming more personally involved, with clear responsibilities and freedom to contact each other as needed.

This system was not without costs. Performing this function well was burdensome and took teacher time away from curriculum develop-

---

[5]This occurred at other schools associated with other design teams, but not as systematically. For example, one of the AT schools had adopted this system and interviews showed the same results, but the majority of AT schools had not adopted it during our visits.

ment or other tasks. Schools recognized this and were in the process of restructuring and setting priorities to ensure its further support.

New Teacher and School Evaluation as Professional Development

Examining a school's performance against standards was helpful, but it was not enough. Sometimes an outside view was needed or a more personal experience, such as gauging a teacher's performance against new standards of delivery as part of the evaluation process. Several teams introduced mechanisms that provided such views and school staff found these to be strong stimulants toward improvement.

Critical Friends. CON created a critical friends team to visit and evaluate the progress of its schools toward the design, to offer recommendations, and to hear responses. The team changes for each site. It is made up of external education experts as well as school staff from the CON sites not being visited. In this way, staff members from each school get to visit other CON schools. The visit is extensive and takes place over a week with in-depth observation of classrooms.

Teachers who went as critical friends to visit other sites found this to be a very rewarding experience. It encouraged them both to better understand what they were trying to accomplish and to bring information about interesting practices back to their own schools. Importantly, this was the first time most teachers had acted as evaluators. They reported that this experience gave them a more critical eye for what is happening in their own school.

The critical friends report their findings to the school staff as a whole and the staff must then work to come up with remedies for any shortcoming. Again, teachers said that this was an important experience for them because the judgments made by teachers from other schools could not be denied. The exercise was taken very seriously.

Review of School Improvement Plans. Several designs (AT, CON, and NA) require that schools develop descriptive data about their schools, create school improvement plans, and review the plans each year. Often, this was a rather mundane exercise, perhaps because schools and their staff are used to submitting data without really examining them for meaning. However, in the case of NA the plans are submitted to the design team and a rubric is used to judge them. Some sites reported that this provided an impetus to make the plans more meaningful.

New Evaluation. By the end of Phase 2, several schools were beginning to reassess the evaluation of teachers within the school. Sometimes this was part of a formal process.[6] For example, the MRSH and NA designs promote this type of activity. In other cases, it has grown more organically from the other changes taking place in the school (AC, CLC, CON, and RW). As staff at an AC site indicated, "If we are going to teach to 'purpose,' then we should be judged on that." In these instances the governing committee of the school usually reviewed the evaluation form. Often, it was easy to gear the form to the new goals of the school and begin to evaluate teachers' and administrators' performances against their ability to meet design goals. A CLC site offered the most developed form of this process with teachers, parents, and students involved in teacher evaluation. The site has used this new process to remove teachers.

For the most part, teachers said they did not want to evaluate other teachers. They would like input into the criteria for evaluation, making sure they were consonant with design goals, but they did not want the responsibility for them. That tended to remain with principals. Two exceptions are the EL and MRSH designs, which encouraged teachers to peer-review the curriculum units developed. This procedure was in its infancy at the time of the last visits. CLC also offered exceptions to this tendency.

Getting Networked. MRSH insisted that teachers review their own curriculum. To support this activity, all curriculum was entered into the networked computer system that outlined scope and sequence, where units were placed, and what assessments had been developed. At the end of Phase 2, teachers had just been trained on this equipment and software. The excitement engendered was high. For the

---

[6]Rosenholtz (1989) indicates the importance of matching the evaluation to shared values within the school. In her quantitative analysis of contributions to shared goals, changed teacher evaluations make the largest contribution, second only to teacher socialization (partly developed through teaming). Evaluating teachers by the goals of the design further works to confirm and internalize the goals in teachers' minds and practice.

first time, they could effectively share curriculum across grades, see what other grades were doing, and make comments as appropriate. At the two elementary schools we visited, teachers reported that this curriculum and instructional management capacity was beginning to significantly increase sharing among teachers across all levels and also to encourage peer review of practices. Teachers could provide specific instances of this—especially of talking with teachers at different grade levels, which had not been the norm in the school before.

Challenges to New Visions of Professionalism

We would like to report that this move toward professionalism will result in permanent changes, and that it can be easily adopted by other schools. But it has several hurdles to cross.

- The activities outlined fly in the face of expectations and normal professional development planning of schools and districts. They confront head-on the notion that a simple workshop will provide the desired change in student outcomes or that significant changes in professional development can be accomplished within a year.

- District officials expected that several of the efforts, most especially the notion of changed teacher evaluations, would be opposed by teachers' unions.

- The activities outlined take time and resources not often dedicated to teachers. In our last interviews, several schools noted that district budget cuts would reduce these activities in the future.

- None of the NASDC teams have adequately involved teachers' colleges in this effort to reformulate the profession. Within the confines of the NASDC deadlines and goals, teams had difficulty managing school change as well as reaching out to teachers' colleges to effect better training and a redefinition of the job of teaching. Teachers will continue to arrive at school doors unprepared for the type of responsibility, authority, and work that is becoming the province of teachers associated with NASDC schools.

In general, short time lines, budget pressures, and the vastness of the existing system raise strong barriers to the types of changes the teams attempted to engender.

NEW VISIONS OF SCHOOL AUTONOMY

We have stated in other parts of this report that design teams did not achieve the full vision of school autonomy that they described in their proposals. We indicated that one reason for this was that the team and school did not have sufficient influence to gain that autonomy. Here we argue that autonomy itself might not be a sufficient condition for reform; one must also know how to use autonomy. This implies a learning period by schools and districts, which implies a significantly longer time frame for reform than allowed the NASDC schools.

The teams differed in their approach to gaining the autonomy that they felt was needed by schools. Several design teams made strong statements about the need for large concessions to the schools in terms of control over budgets, staffing, hiring, and firing. They entered into negotiations with sites to ensure that the schools received the authority to make those decisions. For example, NA argued that all schools should have control of 85 percent of their budgets, and CLC and MRSH argued for full control by the schools over staffing decisions. The problem with these ambitious goals was that neither design teams, schools, nor districts articulated what would occur if the school had that authority. But, by asking for that authority, much staff time and negotiation energy was spent going over legal issues, worst-case scenarios, etc., with little produced. This finding is in keeping with other research that notes that site-based management does not succeed when it becomes an end in itself (Murphy and Hallinger, 1993; Turnbull, 1985; Wohlstetter, 1995).

Other design teams required fewer initial concessions. For example, RW required only that the school have discretion over its Chapter 1 funding. Or as schools associated with other teams began to transform themselves, devoting energy to curriculum, instruction, standards and assessments, and other concrete changes, it became increasingly obvious that limited authority over budget, staffing, and personnel decisions prevented the attainment of goals. For example, it became clear for schools associated with AC, CON, and RW that lack of school-level control over the "resource" teacher positions would prevent the schools from allocating the existing personnel to positions needed to help maintain the design. Alternatively, some schools argued that one or two teachers simply did not buy into the design and were holding up the implementation effort. They wanted authority to transfer these teachers. Without this limited authority, they thought the reforms would not progress in the next year. Finally, all schools found that they needed releases from existing assessment systems.

By the end of Phase 2 some sites, no matter which design, had developed enough toward design goals that they could now understand the need for very specific authorities at the school level and develop their own specific arguments for being allocated those powers. Perhaps just as important, some were using authorities that they always had but had never before taken advantage of. In several instances, the district insisted that the school had always had the power to make certain staffing decisions, but that the principals had not chosen to exercise it. In short, a change in attitude came with the development of the site toward concrete design goals. Growing commitment to design principles and seeing the effects of real applications allowed schools to mature in their ability to use existing powers and argue for more power and authority.

It would be nice to credit the designs with this change, but in fact, it was coming about because of changes in the districts as well. In several cases, the districts had begun to adopt site-based management reforms that encouraged schools to ask for more authority.[7]

As we left sites in spring 1995, the following was occurring in our sample of 35 schools:

---

[7]We visited 15 districts. Of these, the schools we studied in three districts were charter schools or magnets with special autonomies granted (Minneapolis, Jefferson, and New York). Those in Fond du Lac were under Native American control. In addition, the schools in Jefferson and Calloway Counties were part of the Kentucky Education Reform Act site-based management movement that preexisted NASDC. Of the remaining 10 districts, seven had made moves toward site-based management during the NASDC Phase 2 and attributed some of this move to working with the design team, or schools associated with design teams were covered by these new initiatives: Los Angeles, Worcester, Columbus, San Diego, Dubuque, Prince George's County, and Indianapolis.

- Thirteen schools had clear control over non-staff-related funds in the school budget. However, most had this power for reasons other than working with design teams: four were charter or magnet schools, two were LEARN schools in Los Angeles, three were under KERA, and three were part of the Challenger Initiative with Prince George's County.[8] Another 12 schools were explicitly negotiating agreements concerning this control.

- Thirteen schools were negotiating with their district to have greater internal control over staffing positions, such as the ability to substitute between instructional aides and classroom materials, substituting nonclassroom personnel for classroom personnel, or substituting categories of nonclassroom personnel such as a reading teacher for a computer support aide. Schools associated with six design teams now have authority to make their own hiring decisions outside the district pool. In Prince George's County, the district gave the school authority to hire a new principal.

- Although almost all schools talked of the need to fire or transfer personnel who did not support the design, to our knowledge only one had done so for reasons directly related to support of the design. At least seven had this authority.

From this we learn a simple lesson. Specific school autonomy is essential to reform, but it is perhaps best to back into it. It is the working of design teams, sites, and districts together over time that eventually permitted a reallocation of authority to lower levels. If allowed to grow into it, schools that have gone through a maturing period can find effective uses for that power.

This observation emphasizes the need for an extended horizon when attempting school reform. We must look to several additional years beyond the initial two provided by NASDC for schools to gain the autonomy needed by designs and to learn to use it effectively to promote improved student outcomes. It also emphasizes the large barrier to reform embedded in the existing decisionmaking structures of school districts.

---

[8]Recall that the design teams chose schools that did have these authorities precisely because those authorities would promote the design.

CONFLICTING CULTURAL NORMS BETWEEN SCHOOLS AND DESIGNS

We must report that despite the best efforts of design teams to engage schools in reforms and to actively support the school staff in achieving reforms, some sites and designs simply were not good matches. We did not see a pattern in this, such as urban schools being unable to adopt a particular design whereas rural ones could. Such a pattern might exist, but it was not observable because of the limited number of observations (two sites) for any one team.

We found that mismatches were related to conflicting missions between the design and the school. A few examples will indicate the nature of the problem as manifested in Phase 2. In addition, we found much slower progress in middle schools and high schools. Both types of conflicts—mismatches in visions, and difficulties in reform in the higher grades—point to a longer time frame needed in certain instances for overcoming barriers, but also show that some specific interventions might be needed for certain constituencies.

Talented and Gifted Programs and Designs for All Students

All of the designs are based on the notion that they will improve the performance of all children and that all children can learn. To ensure that this happens, they often change the nature of student assignments to classrooms and within classrooms.[9]

By and large, schools associated with the designs were implementing these changes. They faced barriers, but not insurmountable ones. Many teachers support inclusionary models, at least in theory, and were willing to work toward them when properly supported. In addition, many of the districts that NASDC teams worked with were heading in the direction of inclusionary strategies and thus supported the teams. The main issue appeared to be that teachers felt that they could not handle the inclusionary models within their classroom while carrying a large student load. They argued for

---

[9]For example, EL requires multi-year teaching and mainstreaming of special-needs children, CON requires multi-year and multi-age teaching, and RW requires reassignment of students based on an assessment performed every eight weeks and mainstreaming of special-needs students.

smaller student loads or for new student management practices to support the new groupings. Some teams (CON and RW) gave strong support to teachers in this area and the teachers report that class-rooms appear to be working well, despite teachers' initial misgivings.

However, in some specific instances the design and school were in strong conflict over this issue and remain deadlocked. This was the case if both parents and teachers with vested interests in the talented and gifted (TAG) programs acted to protect their interests and other teachers were not engaged in a dialog concerning this central issue. These programs are essentially exclusionary and are governed by strong supporting legal frameworks, rules, regulations, and resource assignments.

Throughout the two-year period, we interviewed parents, usually chosen by the administrators or design teams to represent the views of parents at large. It was often the case that some of these were par-ents of talented and gifted children who made a special effort to visit with us to present their views of what was happening in the schools. And their view was not supportive. TAG parents, as we have come to know them, were concerned about the reforms taking place and worried that their children would be denied the special resources that had at one time been funneled to them. The discussion often centered around "cooperative groupings" in the classroom where the excelling students were expected to work with those less adept. Not only that, but the excelling students were expected to tutor or aid their peers when needed. Parents of TAG children or of generally well-performing students were concerned that their children's time was being taken up with irrelevant nonsense and that their children were being held back by having to support "the less able" ones. In contrast, all parents of special education students we interviewed were supportive of the changes being made and willingly testified that inclusionary programs has increased their children's perfor-mance.

These contrasting views were expressed by at least some parents at every site, but were not enough to form a barrier unless combined with other factors—namely, teachers whose status in the school rested on the continuation of these programs. The clearest example of this was in an urban high school whose reputation rested on its magnet status. The school's magnet status came as a result of the district's desegregation plan, which included a TAG program to draw white and Asian students into the majority black school.

The design that the school accepted is dedicated to inclusionary policies, yet the responsibility for implementation of the design was given to the head of the TAG program. The parts of the design that would change the status of the TAG program are completely ignored and the school still runs two separate and unequal tracks.

Parents we talked with from the school supported the magnet program—but these were all parents whose students were in it. During our visits, we were shown to magnet classes and to a fair put on by the magnet students. When directly asked whether the school would be changing the student assignment pattern, the TAG teachers said it would not.

In several other sites, this pattern repeated itself, but not so obviously or blatantly. In one site associated with a TAG program, parents and teachers were set against the design until test results showed increases in student performance across the board, including the TAG children. In another, teachers refused to implement multi-year groupings because "that type of thing is for students with problems." Teachers refused to implement the new student grouping.

We cannot attest to whether these groupings, when implemented, will prove efficacious in the ways design teams propose. We can report that in some schools they face a fundamental barrier in that they threaten programs and constituencies that have prospered under the existing system.

Other Mission or Environmental Conflicts

Similar types of conflict arose between the school's view of itself and the design team vision, as did conflict because of changed environments.

In general, within our sample, high schools showed less progress toward design goals than did elementary or middle schools. This was expected for two reasons, which were borne out in our interviews.[10] First, high schools are traditionally organized around disciplines and teachers have been trained in those particular disciplines. In addition, content tends to become more abstract and theoretical in high school than in elementary schools. Thus, teachers in high school are less amenable to changes in curriculum and instruction that promote interdisciplinary, hands-on activities. Second, high schools are closer to colleges and must produce graduates that are acceptable to colleges as judged by standardized assessments. The barriers presented to the designs by graduation requirements, standardized tests, and college entrance exams were formidable. These are part of the culture of high schools that will be very difficult to change.

New schools created in response to NASDC, or simply newly established, had a difficult time making progress toward the NASDC reforms simply because they had formidable obstacles in terms of growth and administrative issues within the first few years of existence that drained energies away from reform. The culture of a new school, while in some ways pliable, is at the same time often chaotic and inhospitable to reasoned change and reform. The experiences of new schools associated with CON, EL, and CLC proved this out.

High schools offering extensive electives did not buy into design teams' notions of "less is better," a basic or core curriculum for all students, or concentrated studies. Conflicts appeared between the AT and MRSH designs and their high school sites over this issue. At one AT high school, the teachers flatly refused to consider reducing the number of electives.

Charter and reservation schools associated with CLC faced a different set of cultural conflicts. These schools, because of environmental factors, experienced frequent staff turnover, which reduced the ability to make permanent changes. The charter schools were formed by strong-willed teachers to get away from administrative structures and to institute their own particular brand of reforms. Reservation schools had strong missions to protect specific cultures and were

---

[10]The specific difficulties of changes in high schools are described in Powell et al. (1985). Difficulties in moving to an interdisciplinary curriculum are described in Bodilly et al. (1995). The Coalition of Essential Schools, which focuses on changing high schools, has noted difficulties as well (McDonald, 1995; Sizer, 1992).

caught up in the politics of the tribe. Administrators in these schools held strong opinions about the visions of their schools that sometimes conflicted with the CLC design. Furthermore, these schools, even though they had distinctive autonomy, were not free from political pressures within their own communities. When added to the newness of the charter schools in the CLC sample, these findings explain some of the difficulties in progress encountered by the CLC design in the sample we chose.

Several schools in the sample had embraced other reform visions before becoming associated with NASDC design teams and had difficulty letting go of the past visions and accepting the new one. The EL school in New York City associated with multiple other reforms and the NA school in San Diego associated with a Comer model were two prime examples of this. In cases like this the school had to make a choice. It could not effectively serve two masters.

School Culture as Barrier

Design teams faced a particular set of difficulties in overcoming cultural norms in schools that were wedded strongly to particular missions, that served particular students to the exclusion of others, or that embraced a reform in conflict with the design. The existing culture of the school proved very strong, at least in the short run, and progress was often stalled because of it, contributing to the uneven pace of reform across schools. These experiences reinforce the need for a better selection process in matching design teams and schools and accepting an extended horizon for change when facing certain barriers.

COMMUNITY INVOLVEMENT/PUBLIC ENGAGEMENT AS AN ESSENTIAL PART OF REFORM

A theme running through the above discussion is the difficulty of schools and their staff to make connections to those outside the school. It manifested itself in the inability of the design teams and schools to effect strong changes in social services, governance, teachers' colleges, higher education, and existing assessment systems that constrict schools in pursuit of their missions.

Design teams all insisted that they would address public engagement or community involvement. And some did take on this element to produce a narrow change. For example, several designs insist that students perform community service, as much to help students understand their place in society as to encourage the community to take a greater part in the school. Others, such as CON, EL, LALC, and RW, greatly increased the volunteers in the school and the involvement of different community groups in tutoring, lecturing, or mentoring students. These programs probably produced solid good in the school and we look forward to the full evaluation of their effect on student outcomes.

However, this blossoming of community involvement in the schools addressed only a narrow, though rather traditional for schools, conception of the issue of "public engagement." Universally, design teams are concerned that they have not effectively involved the public in discussion of the goals of schooling, the attributes of graduates, how graduates should be judged, or even the value of education. With few marginal exceptions, they did not involve, to the extent necessary for the changes demanded, those quasi-public or quasi-governmental bodies that control schools, such as organizations that provide standardized tests, teachers' colleges that provide new recruits to schools, or universities and colleges that prescribe the seat time requirements for curriculum, etc.

The design teams are aware of this and are equally aware that singly they lack the ability to affect these larger entities. NASDC is now promoting a collective push toward this goal.

IMPLICATIONS

Previous chapters, because they held to the more absolute NASDC standard of full demonstration, indicated that the teams did not accomplish all that NASDC intended within the two-year period. In fact, teams argued from the beginning that substantial changes in the culture of the school would not take place in the two-year time period they had been given. This chapter notes some of the barriers to the cultural changes attempted. However, some of those important changes were beginning to occur by the end of Phase 2 and the teams carried some major responsibility for helping them occur. They had not been completed yet, but our findings indicate that many sites were in the process of establishing very important changes in professional development and school autonomy. They were less successful in overcoming issues involving alternative assessments and gaining community support.

The implications for Phase 3 are positive—these types of changes can be introduced and promoted by agents external to schools. The implication for more general reform is that these changes do take time. In particular, there appears to be an organic nature to them. An external agent can introduce and support them, but the school staff itself must learn to embrace them and then argue with the powers that be for changes. The move of some design teams at the end of Phase 2 into more systemic issues is part of an unfolding reform movement. These are symptoms of new organizations, growing in organic fashion, looking for a toehold in the larger system that will allow them to fulfill their missions.

However, several barriers, especially embedded cultures that conflict with design norms, the use of conflicting assessments, and the inability of schools to tackle issues of public engagement, remain to be overcome.

Chapter Seven

LESSONS LEARNED ABOUT DESIGN-BASED ASSISTANCE ORGANIZATIONS AS AGENTS OF SCHOOL REFORM

To conclude this formative assessment of NASDC's Phase 2, we move away from comparing the accomplishments and goals of specific teams. Instead we reflect on the lessons learned from the NASDC Phase 2 experience in general. In enumerating these lessons, we stretch the evidence somewhat to avoid weak statements, but we believe that this stretch allows us to make important points succinctly. We then use these lessons to construct the characteristics of a proto- type, design-based assistance organization that might act success- fully as a change agent for reform in schools.

LESSONS LEARNED

Formative assessment of the NASDC Phase 2 experience falls prey to a perception problem captured in the 1960s national advertisement campaign for the Peace Corps, "is the glass half empty or half full?" Judging by the NASDC Phase 2 experience, pessimists might feel that school-level reform is difficult if not impossible, because several teams did not meet the NASDC goals. Optimists, on the other hand, might find the results encouraging by focusing on what teams were able to accomplish, given the ambitiousness of the goals when com- pared to past experience with school reform.

We draw a different lesson from the experience, which involves the setting of proper expectations for progress specific to the types of reforms attempted in the different elements of schooling. We believe that the findings of this study should countermand the tendency noted in Adelman and Pringle (1995, p. 29):

> Most mainstream administrators, school boards, and taxpayers underestimate how much time is needed for school faculty members to individually and collectively imagine and examine radically different conditions of schooling; to coordinate efforts to experiment with these new conditions; to reflect on and evaluate these experiments and to institutionalize the most worthwhile, discard the unacceptable, and refine the rest, and to maintain simultaneously the daily functioning of the school.

The evidence provided indicates that some types of changes in schools, when supported by design teams with strong assistance strategies, can take place within a two-year time frame. Other elements, no matter the team or level of effort, appear to take longer. Some types of changes cannot be accomplished by design teams alone. The challenge remaining for the teams is to extrapolate from their Phase 2 experience a reasonable set of expectations for progress and a rational sequence of implementation activities for arriving at whole-school transformation toward improved student outcomes.

In support of this general notion, we note the following specific lessons:

- Within the short period of time allowed by NASDC, progress depended heavily on the readiness of teams to undertake their mission. Readiness was indicated by a team staffed to produce the changes proposed, a fully developed design with concrete models to offer sites, and an implementation strategy geared toward strong support and assistance to school personnel. As teams develop this capacity, they should become stronger forces for change.

- Within a short period of time, concentration on change in the core elements of schooling appeared to have highest payoff. Sites floundered when they took on too much too soon.

- Site development approaches were valuable because they helped school staff incorporate cultural changes through new methods of professional development, but it must be understood that this approach takes longer and works better when the school has excess capacity to devote to the effort.

- Some elements simply are not predisposed to quick implementation and develop at a different pace than others, most especially those that require coordination with external actors who are not at the beck and call of schools (social service integration) or those that require a process of learning by multiple actors (changed governance structures and public engagement). Importantly, some changes in these areas are necessary for the institutionalization of each of the designs and cannot be avoided in the long term.

- The capability of the design teams to provide concrete assistance to all personnel was crucial in producing change, emphasizing the need for such external sources of assistance.

  — Initial efforts to produce school-level commitment were not fortuitous, but methods for improving in this area are under way. Stronger commitment was obtained and progress made by continued support and effort by the teams, arguing for the important role of assistance.

  — Assistance must reach all school personnel, be provided over a significant period of time, and provide concrete models, materials, coaching and facilitation, and teaming opportunities.

  — The level of assistance cannot be supported without significant resources. Those resources will vary by teams and school.

  — Even strong implementation strategies and assistance will not reduce the time needed for some changes, but they might make change more probable and more apparent.

- Many barriers to the process of school transformation exist, especially in the areas of professional development, school autonomy, and conflicting cultural values and assessments that work against change. These barriers require stronger public engagement by design teams and schools, but even this would not overcome the lack of influence over important actors that is missing from the "design team" model of school transformation. So far, whole-school designs and design-based assistance are limited vehicles to reform and must be coupled creatively with other efforts.

Given the above, the major lesson learned is to set realistic goals for change and recognize that different changes take different amounts of time and resources. Too ambitious an agenda for change leaves the audience for reform disappointed in the interim results. Too meek an agenda for change leaves the audience disappointed as well. Well-articulated phasing strategies might be the best way to garner support and accomplish the ultimate goals of improved student outcomes.

Setting realistic expectations for change will become increasingly important to the NASDC design teams as they enter new sites and necessarily address the internal issue of building increased capacity to service more sites.

BROADER ACCOMPLISHMENT IN REFORM AGENDA

At this point in time, the distinctive contribution of NASDC to educational reform has been to help capitalize and support a mechanism for the building of school-level capability for transformation: a design-based assistance organization. In this sense, NASDC's efforts can be seen as a capacity-building policy (McDonnell and Grubb, 1991). The notion of a design-based, assistance organization is a set of propositions arrived at inductively but supported by the Phase 2 experiences of the design teams and sites, which indicated the necessary attributes of the organizations that could most effectively aid schools in transformation. We propose that a design-based assistance organization should have the following attributes:

- A capable, well-staffed design team that understands and supports the tenets of the design.
- A fully developed design that communicates effectively the vision and specific tasks of school reform advocated by the team.
- A proven implementation strategy and capability to provide assistance over time.

- The existence of demonstration sites to act as further laboratories of reform and to provide hands-on evidence of success.

These attributes are possible only with a strong resource base. The following paragraphs explore each of these propositions in more detail.

A Capable, Well-Staffed Design Team That Understands and Supports the Tenets of the Design

A capable team would include a stable and established leader or set of leaders, an experienced staff dedicated to the ideas of the design and capable of serving the needs of sites, and, when called for, the proven working partnerships described by the design vision. The design team experts would be able to provide inservices to the school staff on the uses of the materials, models, and the processes for change. This implies that the design team successfully develops its own people or relies on competent contractors who understand and support the tenets of the design.

A Fully Developed Design That Communicates Effectively the Vision and Specific Tasks of School Reform Advocated by the Team

In every case, the vision of the NASDC teams is student-centered and standards-based, but each team uniquely expresses and emphasizes different functions, purposes, and missions of the school. The vision of a design is often found in the focus on *student expectations* with clear and specific goals for education. Those goals are communicated through many means including definitive standards, strategic planning processes, and curriculum and instruction packages.

The provision of concrete materials expressing the design details helps teachers work through the process of change and guides their efforts toward demonstrating design elements. These models should include not just curriculum and instruction, but new infrastructure, new scheduling options, new budgeting processes, etc. Team development or site development approaches should both be described in concrete form, with documentation and specific applications that site-level staff can understand and use. In the end, it is the completeness of the package of models and materials that communicates the full vision of whole-school reform.

An essential part of this package is a self-critical, feedback mechanism to the school, which creates the dissonance between desired outcomes and current outcomes needed to motivate change. Every model of organizational change begins with the introduction of a performance gap as essential to motivating people toward change and ends with a continuous feedback loop that promotes continued change. We found that design teams that had successfully inserted a meaningful self-examination into the school organization could show that this component had some likelihood of sustaining the school over time, after a strong design team presence left. This self-critical component manifested itself in different ways:

- Well documented and understood standards and school assessment components.

- Strategic planning processes that collected and reviewed performance information in an on-going basis.

- Visits from teams of colleagues from other schools and outside experts as "critical friends" to review progress made by the site and point out weaknesses and strengths.

- Visits by school staff to schools with characteristics common to their own and that were considered by the team to be excellent schools.

- Facilitators associated with design teams, or design team personnel who acted in a similar capacity, to point out weaknesses and strengths and the means for improving according to the design tenets.

- Continued expectations for change communicated by the design team members in their site visits.

A Proven Implementation Strategy and Capability to Provide Assistance over Time

An assistance organization should have a proven implementation strategy, or set of strategies, which would include: (a) a plan for choosing new sites and introducing the design effectively; (b) a capability to define effectively the relationship between the sites and team; (c) the ability to provide information to the sites through the exchange of materials, conferences, inservices, and use of facilitators, etc.; (d) the ability to support the sites in changing the infrastructure of the schools, such as new scheduling plans, needed committees, new teacher evaluations, new staffing assignments; (e) the capability to lead sites through a quality-control process that would ensure that the design was implemented by all teachers and reached all students; (f) feedback from practitioners that the approach has proved helpful and resulted in improved outcomes; and (g) access to resources to support this work.

The provision of a quality-control mechanism that would ensure that all teachers and students were performing well is essential. This is closely related and perhaps inseparable from the self-critical feedback loop. It stands apart only to indicate that teachers need specific feedback on their products, such as curriculum units or classroom delivery, to determine quality in the sense that those products meet the design expectation. This is different from assessment data that might indicate whether or not the school was improving. At the end of Phase 2, teams were beginning to develop these mechanisms including:

- Processes for teachers to use standards and assessments to effectively change their curriculum and for schools to review curriculum alignment across grades.

- Processes to review all teacher-developed curriculum for quality.

- Development of common rubrics to be used by all teachers.

- Specific examples of student products and their scoring.

- Changed teacher evaluation structures that focused on the tenets of the design.

- Coaching opportunities for teachers failing to implement the design.

- Processes to remove teachers who were not dedicated to the design principles.

The Existence of Demonstration Sites to Act as Further Laboratories of Reform and to Provide Hands-On Evidence of Success

For Phase 3, the final characteristic of a design-based, assistance organization is access to strong demonstration sites. Design teams and sites have argued that this is important for several reasons:

- Credibility—Potential sites must be able to see that the team can deliver on its promises before they agree to try the design.

- Implementation—New partner sites need access to a pool of administrators and teachers who have already transformed their schools and who can give them specific and practical assistance.

- Continual progress—The demonstration sites can continue the progress toward the design vision and eventually prove out the full design with firm evaluation.

Teams and their sites had developed firm notions about this and were actively moving forward with their districts to support work and spread at least portions of the design to other schools or the whole design to other districts.

IMPORTANT, BUT LIMITED, ROLE OF DESIGN-BASED ASSISTANCE ORGANIZATIONS

If fully developed over the next few years, this type of assistance for schools could prove to be a powerful impetus toward improved student outcomes in many schools. However, it does not present the only intervention or a complete picture of needed reform efforts.[1]

The usefulness of the design-based assistance organization appears limited to school- and perhaps district-level changes. Important actors with strong systemic influence on schools remain outside these teams' and NASDC's ability to influence. These are quasi-governmental bodies, higher-level governmental bodies, assessment organizations, teachers' colleges, schools of higher education, and the general public.

---

[1]See Smith and O'Day (1990) for a review of all the other needed changes.

The ability of NASDC to influence change at a more systemic level will be put to the test in Phase 3 as NASDC enters into agreements with a small group of jurisdictions to work toward school-level transformation for more that 30 percent of those districts' schools within a five-year period.

NASDC's FUTURE EFFORTS

Phase 3 is now being planned and initiated. An RFP was sent to jurisdictions in spring 1995. Jurisdictions responded with short proposals and NASDC is now negotiating with these jurisdictions focusing on systemic changes to the operating environment that will be conducive to the success of the design teams in transforming schools. Each of the seven teams plans on entering new school sites in fall 1995 and continuing its demonstration projects in Phase 2 sites.

If NASDC's effort continue as planned, the experiences will form the basis for exploring the ability of teams to truly affect school transformation, and thus to affect student outcomes. It also will afford the chance to more closely examine whether and how NASDC and its design teams operate when the district is supportive of governance changes and the removal of barriers to reform. Finally, it will be a test of whether design-based assistance organizations can create a market for combined design and assistance services that sustains the teams over time without further NASDC subsidization.

DESCRIPTIONS AND DESIGNS

The following descriptions of the designs rely primarily on the elements defined in Chapter Two. The elements are used as appropriate. The design teams described their designs in 50-page documents and dedicated the development year to specifying the details of the designs. Although these brief paragraphs do not do justice to the designs, we hope they capture some of the essential traits of each.

ATLAS: AUTHENTIC TEACHING, LEARNING, AND ASSESSMENT OF ALL STUDENTS (AT)

This design assumes that high-performing schools are not possible in the current bureaucratic structure. The intent of the design is to move schools away from "the bureaucratic reality to the authentic vision" of education. The design aims to change the culture of the schools to promote high institutional and individual performance. Four beliefs about the purpose of schools drive the design. Schools are to:

- Help students acquire valuable habits of heart, mind, and work;

- Help students develop deep understandings;

- Use only activities that are developmentally appropriate; and

- Create a community of learners.

Design Team Leaders: James Comer, Janet Whitla, Howard Gardiner, Sid Smith, Edwin Campbell, and Theodore Sizer.[1]

Governance: The concept of an autonomous pathway is the key to the design because it frees a contiguous group of schools from constrictive governance structures. Equivalent to a feeder pattern that is coterminous with a community, the pathway must be self-governing, requiring formal changes in the governance structure of the district. Schools within a pathway will be formally governed by a School Planning and Management Team (SPMT). This team will be supported by school-level teams, a Community Health Team, a Teacher Team, a Parent Program, and a Student Program in each school. All will work to support the SPMT. Members will represent different important voices in the community, making governance more participatory. Decisions will be made by consensus with free, no-fault discussion guided by a process developed by the School Development Program. The pathway will be governed by the ATLAS Community Team (ACT) and use the same consensus processes.

Standards: Using the new governance structure, each pathway will rethink what a high school graduate should be able to do. From this reconception, it will develop its own standards of performance for each grade level through the committees. Standards will be performance- and outcome-based. They will be explicitly stated and public so that the community can join in judging the efficacy of the schools.

Assessments: The pathway creates exemplary exhibitions for graduates and benchmarks for key years. Assessments are authentic in that they must be demonstration- and performance-based. There is strong support for portfolios to be used over time to demonstrate student development and maturation.

Student Groupings: The design will promote multi-age grouping as appropriate and will avoid pullout programs. Tracking will be avoided.

Curriculum and Instruction: The curriculum moves away from emphasis on accumulating a broad set of facts to emphasize in-depth

---

[1]Linda Gerstle replaced Sid Smith in spring 1995.

understanding of the world. For example, in high school, many elec-tives and lecture formats would be changed to fewer courses with more in-depth experiences. Curriculum is organized by themes called "essential questions." Answers to the questions are explored in an interdisciplinary fashion. Instruction is highly personalized with attention to individual capabilities and maturation rates. This is reinforced by a personalized school structure with a reduced number of students per teacher.

Professional Development: Teachers become a stronger force in the school by creating their own professional development plans, being responsible for research and development of new curriculum and instructional strategies, and being members of the governance teams. Personalization will be promoted through opportunities for collaboration and support for training including networking among teachers.

Community Involvement: Ancillary services such as mentoring, speakers' programs, and volunteers are provided by community members who become more active. Community members are active participants on the school governing teams and the schools develop programs to encourage parental involvement.

Integrated Social Services: Schools closely coordinate with social service providers through the Community Health Team. Members from this team sit on the SPMT to ensure community health issues are heard.

Staffing: Schools commit to fewer students per teacher such that a high school teacher would have no more than 80 students.

Technology: Computers will be used in the classrooms to aid in per-sonalized instruction. They will also enable communication within schools and across the pathway, cementing the relationships needed to build a community of learners.

AUDREY COHEN COLLEGE SYSTEM OF EDUCATION (AC)

This design is based on a holistic approach to education centered in a developmentally appropriate curriculum. Curriculum and instruc-tion are organized around a single, developmentally appropriate purpose for each semester, cumulating to 26 purposes in a K–12 system. For example, kindergarten is dedicated to the exploration of "We build a family-school partnership" and "We care for living things." Embedded in each purpose are content areas such as English and math, and essential skills such as critical thinking and researching. Each purpose culminates in a constructive action undertaken by the class to serve the community. These fundamental changes in the curriculum and instruction become the organizing principles for all other school activities. The total effect is intended to make the school and its programs more coherent and focused.

Design Team Leaders: Audrey Cohen and Janith Jordan.

Governance: Does not require significant governance changes other than those given to magnet or theme schools. However, significant governance changes can result from the incorporation of purposes as the focus of schooling.

Standards: The school will meet existing state standards, but every school will also have the standards developed by the Audrey Cohen College that align and support the purpose-driven curriculum.

Assessments: Although schools continue to use existing standardized tests as required by the district and state, the design team has also developed a framework of demonstrable abilities and skills for each grade. Teacher-developed assessments are embedded in the curriculum and match the specific purpose of each semester. The team is currently working with the sites to develop outcome-based assessment criteria and strategies that incorporate community participation.

Student Grouping: Students will be grouped in ways appropriate to the purpose and constructive action of each semester. The curriculum is intended to promote learning of all students.

Curriculum and Instruction: During each semester, students focus all learning and activities on a single pre-assigned purpose. Traditional subject areas and important skills are absorbed by action-oriented dimensions: acting with purpose, weighing values and ethics, understanding self and others, understanding systems, and making use of skills. The semester culminates in a constructive action that has been determined by the students and is directed toward improving the world outside the classroom. Secondary students serve internships in the community.

Professional Development: The team will provide continued development of teachers in the constructs of the design. Teachers, principals, and administrators organize their jobs around the purposes and begin to build bridges between the school and the outside world.

Community Involvement: The purposes help the school and its officials identify key community resources to involve in the educational enterprise. The constructive actions help bring the community into the school and the school into the community—making schools, parents, and children active partners in improving the community.

Integrated Social Services: The design specifies that coordination with community and health service agencies is accomplished at the site level. The curriculum makes student awareness of health issues and contact with health-related agencies an organic part of the curriculum.

Staffing: The design requires the creation of a staff resource position to gather materials and make contacts in the community, peer-coach teachers in the classroom, and serve as a liaison with the design team. Teachers are responsible for planning the curriculum as a collaborative team. Administrators remove barriers to making the school more coherent and build bridges to the community to support the purposes.

Technology: Networked classroom computer centers, studios for television and photography, and other technology provide students access to information and the means for developing work products. Technology is also applied to the management of record-keeping tasks.

THE CO-NECT SCHOOL DESIGN (CON)

The design calls for a dramatically different learning environment for students, teachers, and the community. The design is especially targeted at middle school children in urban settings; however, it can be applied to other grades and settings. In addition to understanding key subject areas, graduates of the Co-NECT schools demonstrate the acquisition of specific critical skills, identified as sense-maker, designer, problem-solver, decisionmaker, communicator, team worker, product-oriented worker, and responsible, knowledgeable citizen.

Design Team Leaders: Bolt, Berenek, and Newman Associates: John Richards, Bruce Goldberg, and Henry Olds.

Governance: The School Governance Council, which includes teachers, parents, business/community representatives, and administrators, runs the school.   In addition, the school design team provides local input concerning the implementation, performance assessment, and accountability of the Co-NECT approach at that particular school.   Finally, the Community Support Board fosters access to the local community to support the Council and design team.

Standards: The team will develop its own standards with input from the community and with the aid of its associates at Boston College's Center for the Study of Testing, Evaluation, and Education Policy (CSTEEP). Standards will exceed current expectations for middle school students from urban areas.

Assessments: Separate performance assessment frameworks, developed in partnership with CSTEEP, provide the basis for a continuing process of setting goals and measuring progress for individual students, groups, and the school as a whole.

Student Grouping: The school is organized into multi-age, multi-year clusters of students with the goal of low student/teacher ratios.

Curriculum and Instruction: The design features a locally developed, project-based curriculum that is product-oriented and supplemented by seminars and workshops in skills and other areas. Curriculum will be multidisciplinary and will use cluster-wide investigations. Students follow a personal growth plan developed by teachers, parents, and the student.

Professional Development: Professional development is viewed as an ongoing process. Co-NECT teachers promote their own professional development and have access to a network of professional development services and materials. Professional development will be project-oriented with teachers learning by doing.

Community Involvement: A community support board will help the school interact with the community at large. Mentoring and volunteering are encouraged and community input sought for standard-setting.

Integrated Social Services: Counseling and referral will be provided. Teacher teams will work closely with students to provide support.

Staffing: The school will have fewer students per teacher and teachers will remain with students for two to three years. Staff will be organized in multidisciplinary teams in houses.

Technology: A technological infrastructure supports student access to knowledge and local, national, and global resources, the creation of student products, and the management of personal growth plans, resumes, and portfolios.

COMMUNITY LEARNING CENTERS (CLC)

Community Learning Centers are predicated on the school site operating independently from any governmental structure in the areas of budget, staffing, and program. The school is organized into centers and the curriculum and instruction are developmentally based and attuned to students' personal needs. The school becomes a center for learning for all members of the community and promotes access to community services.

Design Team Leaders: John Cairns, Wayne Jennings, Joe Nathan, and Elaine Salinas.

Governance: CLC design is predicated on the need to break the chains of current bureaucracy through an institutional bypass. This translates into very significant site-based decisions, possible at this time only in charter, contract, and reservation schools, or in districts that agree to meet CLC's stipulations. Thus, the design centers around the support of these schools' requirement for full autonomy over budget and the hiring and firing of teachers. The CLC schools would be governed by a site-based council with a collaborative approach to decisionmaking. Over half of the CLC budget goes directly to its sites to support front-end needs for capital and to promote professional development.

Standards: The design does not propose the development of a unique set of standards but insists that all students be held to the same standards that emphasize the demonstration of competencies or performances. These outcome-based standards are intended to be explicit, meaningful, and measurable. The design pledges to ensure that all students have a 75 percent competency rating on existing Minnesota tests and that all students move 25 percentile points on standard measures. The design does promote a standard for ethics as an essential part of character development. This will be developed through close interaction between the student, the school, and the community.

Assessments: The design focuses on the more effective use of different assessment techniques to ensure school accountability, teacher accountability, and accurate student assessment.   It proposes five types of assessments be used to fulfill these different functions. Assessment of students will be more performance-based and will move away from seat-time requirements.

Student Grouping: The design uses groupings appropriate to the learning tasks in a flexible manner. It will emphasize multi-age, multi-year groupings with few pullouts.

Curriculum and Instruction: The design promotes a more interdisciplinary, project-based curriculum and higher-order thinking skills. The point is not to invent new curriculum but to deliver it in ways that make it meaningful to children (instructional strategies). The curriculum emphasizes civic responsibility with students becoming proactive in their communities. Although not requiring specific changes, the curriculum would evolve using modern instructional strategies to be quite different from the current Carnegie units. In consequence, the design requires working with the university system to create new college entry requirements.

A major focus of the design is on the development of new instructional strategies guided by modern principles of learning that call for "brain-based learning." When implemented, these strategies will dramatically increase the learning of all children. The design talks of a paradigm shift from "teaching" to "learning" with student-centered instruction and students being responsible for planning their own curriculum. CLC schools would have a Personal Learning Plan (PLP) for each student, emphasize competency-based education, promote contextual learning and applied real-life problem-solving in areas of interest to the child, pay attention to learning styles and the emotional aspects of learning, and maximize the effective use of technology. Multiple forms of exploration and expression would be used to increase the likelihood of learning.

Professional Development: The design makes strong statements about the need for autonomy to support differentiated staffing and alternative certification to meet the twin goals of equal or less cost than other schools, and an increased staff-to-student ratio required by "brain-based" instructional strategies. Teachers develop professional learning plans in conjunction with a school-wide plan. Each school must commit to giving every teacher 20 days of training a year.

Community Involvement: Schools would be open electronically 24 hours per day to serve adults as well as students. The design has facility plans to translate this into a reality with learning stations located throughout the building. As part of this effort, the team works with the media to increase the attention paid to academic achievement in CLC communities. A collaborative approach is encouraged.

Integrated Social Services: A major thrust is that schools become community centers for learning. Social services would be collocated and coordinated through the schools with special emphasis on preschool services to ensure that children are ready to learn.

Staffing: The intent is for schools to use autonomy over internal resources to significantly restructure the staff, moving teachers toward becoming facilitators of learning and substituting some instructional aides or volunteers for teachers. Older students will guide younger students in their studies.

Technology: The design requires substantial use of computers for student assignment and PLP management, for tracking assessments, and for individualized instructional strategies. Computers and other technologies are used in an integral manner to support learning.

EXPEDITIONARY LEARNING (EL)

The design intends to engage students and revitalize teachers through a teacher-guided, project-based approach to instruction that promotes academic, character, and physical development. The design views schools as institutions that share with families and community in the responsibility to develop students' characters and values. Included are ten design principles of learning, such as students competing against themselves instead of each other to produce a personal best product.

Design Team Leaders: Meg Campbell, Greg Farrell, and Diana Lam.

Governance: The design does not require any formal changes in the governance structure but does advocate a decentralized power structure adopting a web management approach by which administrators provide resources and coordination to meet the specific needs of teachers and the school. School-based management is encouraged.

Standards: Relying on existing national efforts to create standards for various disciplines, the design team is in the process of developing performance standards in the following categories: communication; quantitative reasoning; character and work habits; scientific thinking and technology; cultural, geographic, and historical understanding; arts and aesthetics; and fitness. Each student must complete a senior project.

Assessment: The design calls for authentic assessment, including performance-based exhibitions, student portfolios, and student self-assessment.

Student Grouping: The design eliminates student tracking and mainstreams special education students. Using a multi-year approach, students stay with the same teacher for two to three years to create a more stable teacher-student relationship and to keep the teacher better engaged through the change in grade level every year.

Curriculum and Instruction: The curriculum is based on interdisciplinary, thematic projects, called expeditions, that last from three weeks to a semester. Developed by the teachers who serve as guides rather than repositories of knowledge, each expedition contains intellectual, physical, and service components. Expeditions take place both inside and outside schools and make up about half of the school day. Students continue to receive course work, especially in reading, math, and other basic skills areas.

Professional Development: Staff development is considered the key activity to building a curriculum. The design approach emphasizes treating teachers as professionals by empowering them to create expeditions. Staff development is built around activities that increase the confidence and enthusiasm of teachers, encouraging them to become learners themselves, and that provide teachers with resources and ideas to build curriculum.

Community Involvement: Community involvement is promoted through the off-site nature of the expeditions, the requirement for community service as part of the curriculum, and the need for internships by students. Mentoring and volunteering are promoted.

Integrated Social Services: The design includes a variety of on-site services. The design team intends to reexamine and modify this element in spring 1995, promoting a more site-specific approach to such linkages.

Staffing: Schools will use master teachers and increased teacher differentiation to accomplish their professional development goals. Teachers will be on three-year contracts to match the three-year cycles of multi-year groupings. After each cycle, teachers can choose to continue or to leave. This is intended to promote teacher self-assessment as well as to promote the entry and exit of nontraditional or uncertified teachers. Professional apprenticeships will be encouraged.

Technology: Technology will be incorporated as appropriate.

LOS ANGELES LEARNING CENTERS (LALC)

The Learning Center design calls for significant and substantial changes in instruction and curriculum, school management and governance, and how schools address the health and well-being of students. The design for LALC was created to address the realities of public education in Los Angeles and other urban communities across the nation.

Design Team Leaders: Sid Thompson, Superintendent, Los Angeles Unified School District; Helen Bernstein, President, United Teachers of Los Angeles; Virgil Roberts, President, Solar Records/J. Hines Company; Peggy Funkhouser, President, Los Angeles Educational Partnership; Greta Pruitt, Project Director, Los Angeles Learning Centers.

Governance: Governance and management is designed to ensure that all school community participants are represented in decision-making and that there is an effective infrastructure upon which the Learning Center can build and evolve (includes shared governance, administrators acting as leaders for change, effective communications, ongoing maintenance and renewal, and responsive and flexible management). The school site management council is responsible for budget, personnel, curriculum, community relations, and students' rights.

Standards: The design will make use of the "highest and most nationally recognized" available standards.

Assessment: The Center for Research on Evaluation, Standards, and Student Testing (CRESST) will design a comprehensive student assessment system to improve performance and monitor program effectiveness.

Student Grouping: The design relies on multi-age groupings. The "moving diamond" concept can also be considered a different type of grouping for students, promoting interactions with adults, teachers, and peers.

Curriculum and Instruction: Instruction is designed to ensure that all students are taught in a community of learners using the most effective educational practices. Curriculum content areas include math, science, geography and history, English language arts and the arts, health and fitness, and a second language. Skills and behaviors include effective communication, problem-solving, critical thinking, social cooperation, self-discipline, responsible citizenship, and a lifestyle that values wellness and aesthetics. Curricula for grades 11–12 include job preparation and advanced academic studies. Instruction is expected to reflect current cognitive theories of learning and intelligence, motivations, and individual differences. The designers advocate the following methods: thematic and interdisciplinary instruction, team-teaching, and multi-age classrooms. Teachers receive a prototype "tool box" or library of resources, including curricular units and assessments, that they can use as models to develop their own instructional materials. The design makes use of the "highest and most nationally recognized" available standards. CRESST provides a comprehensive student assessment system to improve performance and monitor program effectiveness. An intensive professional development plan involves teachers in a multi-day training institute focused on curriculum and instruction, enabling, and governance. Management training will be provided to the site leadership team.

Professional Development: The professional development plan involves intensive multi-day training institutes (offered during teachers' off-track weeks) and weekly 1–2 hour training sessions. Much of this is collaborative small-group work with clusters of teachers modeling and coaching each other. Teachers have two hours of pupil-free planning time each week (on the same day, permitting collaborative work). Management training will be provided to the site leadership team.

Community Involvement: Each student is provided with mentors or advocates from among older children, parents or community volunteers, and teachers. These advocates form a team called a "moving diamond" to support the child in his or her educational goals. Town meetings provide parents with a voice in the school.

Integrated Social Services: The LALC refers to this area of work as the "Enabling Component" and expands beyond areas traditionally associated with the integration of health and social services. Enabling is designed to restructure and integrate school community resources to address barriers to student learning. Activities include comprehensive classrooms, school-based and community-linked programs, and services for enabling learning. The design also provides multiple interveners, advocates, and classroom and social supports for students and families.

Staffing: Lead teachers are selected and given the responsibility of assisting individual faculty members and teams in planning new curriculum and redesigning instruction. Leader teachers coach teams, demonstrate lessons, provide sample materials, help faculty solve problems as they arise, and work to implement the instructional efforts. The participation of the teachers' union helps ensure that organization and staffing issues are addressed in a collaborative fashion.

Technology: The three components of the design—instruction, enabling, and management—all use technology to implement the Learning Center design. Technology supports instruction, curriculum development, communication, collaboration, research, text and multi-media publishing, resource access, assessment, administration, and management services. A product development center provides computers, video and audio equipment, laser discs, telecommunications capacity, and other technologies to support multiple instructional learning needs. All teachers have access to portable computers and other technology configurations that they can use daily for instruction, curriculum development, and classroom management. The Learning Centers are linked to the Internet through the Los Angeles Learning Community Network, a low-cost wide-area telecommunications network for teachers.

MODERN RED SCHOOLHOUSE (MRSH)

Several principles and assumptions guide the MRSH design to "break the mold" of American schooling. They include the following:

- Six national goals for education;

- The belief that all students can learn;

- A common culture which is represented by a core curriculum and SCANS[2] generic competencies;

- Principals and teachers with the freedom to organize instruction;

- Schools accountable through meaningful assessments;

- Use of advanced technology to achieving results; and

- Choice in attending a MRSH.

---

[2]Secretary's Commission on Achieving Necessary Skills. See U.S. Department of Labor (1992).

Design Team Leaders: Sally Kilgore and Leslie Lenkowsky.

Governance: The designers require a school plan and school-level autonomy in the areas of budgeting, hiring and staffing, and out-sourcing of services. Multiple teams within the school ensure more teacher participation and the participation of those outside the school.

Standards: The design develops its own unique set of world-class standards for all students that reflect high expectations associated with Hirsch's cultural literacy curriculum for students in the elementary grades and with SCANS competencies and Advanced Placement tests for students in the intermediate and upper grades.

Assessments: Student performance is measured by various assessments, including tests, watershed assessments, and embedded assessments. Schools are expected to adopt MRSH's standards and assessments.

Student Grouping: Design promotes multi-age, multi-year groupings with few pullouts. New instructional strategies will promote individualized instruction and multiple regroupings during project work.

Curriculum and Instruction: The design advocates a curriculum founded on Core Knowledge. Core Knowledge will account for about 50 percent of the curricula, allowing leeway for a school's own curricular emphasis. The elementary students make use of Hirsch's Cultural Literacy curriculum, which is sequenced in a year-by-year fashion. During the second year of Phase 2, the design team plans to develop curricular frameworks for intermediate and upper grade students that reflect MRSH world-class standards. The design conceives of teachers reorganizing instruction thematically across grades, integrating across subjects, and making use of computer technology. Hudson units are a way to "capture" curricular units and connect them into a holistic system of standards, assessments, content, resources, and pedagogy. Students' performance on a "collection" of Hudson units is expected to add up to mastery of MRSH world-class standards. The meaning of "Hudson unit" has evolved over the past six months. Teachers develop Hudson units with guidance by the design team.

The design advocates the more flexible use of time so that all students can meet standards. Instruction would be self-paced. Students would be in heterogeneous, multi-aged clusters with the same teacher for several years. Instruction would emphasize methods to promote student problem-solving and thinking. Acknowledging that all students are capable of learning, albeit at different paces, the MRSH design calls for students to engage in self-paced learning and to organize their learning efforts in accordance with an Individual Education Compact negotiated by the student, parents, and teacher.

Professional Development: The designers conceive of a two-part strategy. The first strategy calls for MRSH to train teachers to implement core features of the design. The other strategy is establishment of a self-sustained professional development program designed at the school level. The details of these strategies are not fully developed; they are to be developed by consultants.

Community Involvement: This is not a heavily emphasized element in the design.

Integrated Social Services: After assessment of a school's community, implementing schools are expected to engage social agencies operating locally to assist "at-risk" pre-kindergarten through grade 12 students. This is a district responsibility, although an expert consultant will facilitate site efforts. The school's primary emphasis will be on education. It is expected that community service agencies will provide their primary emphases.

Staffing: The designers advocate a MRSH teaching force comprising adults from a wide variety of backgrounds made possible by (1) implementing school autonomy over teacher selection and hiring, and (2) curricular change.

Technology: The designers scaled back technology in response to a budget cut (by NASDC) in late spring 1993. The resulting strategy includes a schoolwide computer network and installation of multi-use microcomputers in classrooms. Teachers will use classroom computers to track students' progress through Hudson units and Individual Education Compacts. Students will use the computers for instructional and information access purposes.

NATIONAL ALLIANCE FOR RESTRUCTURING EDUCATION (NA)

Instead of promoting change school by school, the National Alliance provides a framework for all levels of the education system (state and local education agencies as well as schools) to support the restructuring of schools. The vision is based on the belief that systemic change requires a combination of top-down and bottom-up strategies. The Alliance combines member sites and outside experts into a networked umbrella of unifying tasks and goals. It is anticipated that the effort will eventually include about 12 percent of the national student population.

Design Team Leaders: Judy Codding and Marc Tucker.

Standards and Assessments: All National Alliance sites are members of the New Standards Project (NSP), a collaboration of the National Center on Education and the Economy, the National Alliance, and the Learning Research and Development Center at the University of Pittsburgh. The effort goes beyond the National Alliance with a total of 20 states signed on to the project. NSP is both developing new standards as well as incorporating existing high standards in an outcome-based system of assessments.

Alliance sites agree to keep indicators of progress known as Vital Signs to measure whether sites are moving toward the goals of systemic change. Two kinds of measurement are being developed: changes in terms of student performance and indicators of changes in student experiences.

Learning Environments: The design sponsors a number of initiatives aimed at enhancing the curriculum, professional development strategies, and instructional resources to increase learning in schools. The task is an amalgamation of what used to be three separate components of the design: curriculum and instruction, school-to-work focus, and technology as an important part of instruction. The task is intertwined with the NSP in that learning outcomes provide the starting point from which teachers develop units of study that are shared across the Alliance schools. Fundamental to the task is the emphasis on improving the learning environment through professional development opportunities that involve direct interactions among participants and with experts outside the school through a variety of networking devices.

Integrated Social Services: Alliance sites are tasked with developing better ways to integrate health and human services with the schools to serve children's emotional, physical, and academic growth. The task is outcome-based, keyed to agreed-upon descriptions of what communities and schools want for children, such as students coming to school ready to learn.

High-Performance Management: Alliance sites adapt for education the principles and techniques developed by American business known as high-performance management. These include strategic management, human resources management, Total Quality Management, decentralized decisionmaking and empowerment, and accountability and incentive systems. At the school level, principals are trained in these areas to better support the integration and implementation of the design tasks.

Community Involvement/Public Engagement: Alliance sites at the state, district, and school levels are tasked with developing methods for informing and involving parents and the public in the school and restructuring process.

Evolving Design: The specific activities subsumed under each of these tasks continue to evolve; none are in a finished form. For example, a number of activities this year are designed to develop a school-to-work plan and begin working on designs for the high school of the future.

ROOTS AND WINGS (RW)

The design is intended for elementary schools with fairly large allocations of Chapter I funds. The Roots component of the design intends to prevent failure. It emphasizes working with children and their families to ensure that children develop the basic skills and habits they need to do well in succeeding years. The Wings component emphasizes a highly motivating curriculum with instructional strategies that encourage children to grow to their full potential and aspire to higher levels of learning. The means to accomplish both components lies in manipulating existing resources in the school, especially Chapter I funds, to provide better instruction.

Design Team Leaders: Robert Slavin and Nancy Madden.

Governance: The design encourages, but does not require, site-based management under a school improvement team, with the principal acting as Chief Executive Officer. The design relies on the ability of the school to control internal allocations of resources, especially federal and state funds, and staff positions. This requires some understanding between the school, district, state, and federal government about the use of funds. The design team has found few legal barriers to the arrangement.

Standards: The design goal is to improve the performance of all students by raising the average performance and reducing the number of low performers. The design relies on Maryland state tests now in development.

Assessments: Assessments will be increasingly performance-based with hands-on demonstrations and portfolios. The strategy is to position Roots and Wings schools to perform increasingly better on assessments evolving as part of a national move toward improved outcomes, rather than to develop a set of assessment tools unique to Roots and Wings.

Student Grouping: Pullout programs will be eliminated as special teachers, volunteers, and others work in the classroom or after school with students who need additional help. During some parts of the day homogeneous groupings of students will be used for developing specific skills, say, reading skills. Rather than permanent assignment to a group, each student will be assessed and reassigned to new groups as appropriate every eight weeks. The idea is to provide individual attention to those who need it so that they can move from one group to another as they progress. Groupings for math would be different from groupings for reading. During World Lab and other parts of the school day, children will be in heterogeneous groups working in problem-solving modes.

Curriculum and Instruction: The structure of the curriculum will change to encompass three components. First, the schools will use an improved Success for All component for reading and writing skills. The design team is also providing a math component modeled after the reading component and incorporating new standards from the National Council of Teachers of Mathematics. Finally, much of the rest of the day will be devoted to an interdisciplinary, hands-on component called World Lab, which integrates science, social studies, math, language arts, and key skills. Instruction will change dramatically. The problem-solving modes and group learning process will require different teacher instructional styles moving away from lecture formats to that of a guide. Learning will become more activity-based.

Professional Development: The role of the RW facilitator after implementation is to provide release time to teachers, assemble materials, observe teachers' instruction and suggest improvements, and to model the design elements.

Community Involvement: The family support coordinator is responsible for developing volunteers in the schools, structuring the before-school and after-school programs to address individual needs, making home visits to families with children in need, and in general ensuring that children come to school ready to learn.

Integrated Social Services: The focus of ties to the family and community services is on infants, toddlers, and school-age children. Social services will be coordinated through a site-based team run by a family support coordinator at each school (possible through the re-allocation of Chapter I funds) and facilitated by a district move toward more integrated services.

Staffing: The design includes two new staff positions in the school: the family support coordinator, described above, and a Roots and Wings facilitator to ensure that the design is established and maintained.

Technology: The instruction requires additional computer and other resources to provide students with access to hands-on instructional software and educational resources. However, computers are not a central piece of the design.

METHODOLOGY FOR RESEARCH

SAMPLE SITES

Table B.1 shows the sample schools in our design and some important indicators.

EXAMPLES OF APPLYING THE ASSESSMENT CRITERIA

Some simple examples taken from the text will illustrate how we arrived at our assessments and applied the criteria described in Chapter Three.

CURRICULUM

All teams intended to make significant changes to curriculum, based on strong standards, and several steps might logically be involved in this process.

1. The design team defines and specifies the types of changes to be made in documents and through some training.

2. A standards-based curriculum framework, which specifies scope and sequence for learning subjects, is developed by the site or by the team, as appropriate. It is documented.

3. For site-developed designs, the team documents a method for teachers to develop curriculum based on teams' standards. for those favoring student inputs, this is included in the process. For

Table B.1
Characteristics of the Sample Sites

Design Team	School	Grade Span	Enrollment	Free and Reduced-Price Lunch (%)	Setting
AC					
Phoenix, AZ[a]	Loma Linda	K–8	1200	90	Urban
San Diego, CA[b]	Alcott	K–5	395	40[a]	Urban
	Franklin	K–5	540	72	Urban
AT					
Gorham, ME[c,d]	Gorham High School	9–12	500	16[e]	Small city/rural
	Little Falls	K	200	16[e]	Small city/rural
	Narragansett	1–3	473	16[e]	Small city/rural
	Shaw	7–8	340	16[e]	Small city/rural
	Village	4–6	600	16[e]	Small city/rural
	White Rock	1–3	166	16[e]	Small city/rural
Prince George's County, MD	Adelphi[a]	PK–3	505	74	Urban
	Buck Lodge[f]	6–8	675	78	Urban
	Cool Spring[a]	PK–3	540	82	Urban
	High Point[f]	9–12	2117	40	Urban
	Langley Park[a]	4–6	515	92	Urban
CLC					
Cloquet, MN[g]	Fond du Lac	PK–12	231	n/a[h]	Reservation
Duluth, MN[d]	Spotted Eagle	K–6	106	n/a[h]	Small city
Minneapolis, MN[g]	Cedar-Riverside	K–6	82	90	Urban
CON					
Dorchester, MA[i]	Sarah Greenwood	K–6+	348	98	Urban
Worcester, MA[g]	ALL School	K–8	466	80	Urban
EL					
Dubuque, IA	Bryant[g]	K–5	349	26[e]	Small city
	Lincoln[g]	K–5	419	26[e]	Small city
	Central	9–12	162	26[e]	Small city
New York, NY[a]	School for the Physical City	6–8,10	144	38	Urban

Table B.1 (Continued)

Design Team	School	Grade Span	Enrollment	Free and Reduced-Price Lunch (%)	Setting
LALC					
Cudahy, CA[a]	Elizabeth Street	PK–10	2400	88	Urban
Los Angeles, CA[a]	Foshay	K–10	2700	89	Urban
MRSH					
Bartholomew, IN	Columbus East[a]	9–12	1234	8	Small city/rural
	Northside[a]	6–8	805	15	Small city/rural
	Taylorsville[f]	K–6	504	23	Small city/rural
Indianapolis, IN[f]	Frost	K–5	293	60	Urban
NA					
Louisville, KY[a]	Kennedy	K–5	411	66	Urban
Calloway County, KY[g]	Calloway Middle	6–8	727	38[j]	Rural
	Southwest Calloway	K–5	482	37[j]	Rural
San Diego, CA	Darnall[f]	K–5	407	90	Urban
	Marshall[g]	K–5	903	93	Urban
RW					
St. Mary's County, MD[c]	Ridge	PK–5	276	29	Rural
	Lexington Park	PK–5	474	42	Small city

[a]Data approximate as of spring 1995.

[b]Data reported in 1994.

[c]Data reported in 1991.

[d]Grade spans and enrollment as of 1993–1994 site visits.

[e]District-level data, not reported by individual school.

[f]Data reported in 1992.

[g]Data reported in 1993.

[h]These schools operate under the Bureau of Indian Affairs, and meals are provided in a different manner.

[i]The design team ended its relationship with this site during the school year 1993–1994.

[j]Percentage reported as "low-income."

team-developed designs, the team specifies and develops the actual curriculum down to the lesson-plan level. It is documented.

4. Teachers are trained in the curriculum or in the process by which they will create a curriculum, and indicate in interviews that they understand the process.

5. Teachers begin active development of the curriculum, perhaps with students, or active use of the curriculum. In site-developed designs, the new units of study are documented and shared among teachers. At this point, teachers should be familiar with standards, can walk others through the process they are using, and can deliver a unit of study. Enough units of study are developed to fill out the curriculum framework.

6. The newly developed curriculum is reviewed for quality and ability to meet standards across the whole school.

Now let us review what could be observed for two different design teams.

RW: RW provided by the end of Phase 2 a document that explained the three components of its curriculum. The scope and sequence of the curriculum was laid out in keeping with the Maryland state standards and was documented. The team had developed and documented the full curriculum to the lesson-plan level for the improved reading components and for significant parts of the math and World Lab components (several grade levels were missing). Representatives of the district and state had reviewed these materials to help ensure that standards were being met. All teachers had been trained in the developed components. The teachers had the developed materials in their classrooms and were delivering the curriculum. The school staff said that the facilitators were actively coaching them in how best to provide the new curriculum and design team members visited classrooms regularly to help teachers with issues. Teachers provided feedback to the design team about the quality of the curriculum. This held true across the two sites examined. We indicated that RW showed substantial progress and, while slightly behind in the number of units that should have been developed, was generally in keeping with its schedule.

EL: EL had developed a process for teachers to develop their own expeditions (units of interdisciplinary study). All teachers had been trained in this and were given several weeks during the summer of 1993 and again in 1994 to develop expeditions. Most reported that they had begun the development of expeditions and could show us these documents, although this ability varied significantly by site. However, these units were supposed to have been based on a set of standards originally to be delivered by the end of Phase 1. Later, because of difficulties in developing the standards, the schedule was revised so that several standards would be developed and piloted by the end of year 1, Phase 2. In the sites we visited, these standards were not evident at the end of Phase 2 and had not been piloted. Instead sites were using preexisting standards and only beginning the process of review. The number of expeditions developed fell short of the stated requirements of the design team. The design team indicated that a process for review and improvement of the existing units had been developed and was in place in its Denver site and would be replicated at the other sites in fall 1995. We indicated that EL had shown moderate and nonuniform progress on the element of curriculum.

STANDARDS

All teams said they would either accept an existing set of standards, modify an existing set, or develop their own. Again a logical, if not sequential, process toward this goal could be expected.

1. The design team (a) accepted a given set of standards as their own, or (b) modified others or developed their own and documented it in a deliverable.

2. The design team trained teachers in the use of the standards. Teachers can point to a set of standards and say that they have reviewed them and understand the content or performance for their grade level.

3. Teachers began to use the standards to review their curriculum.

4. Groups of teachers and the school began to review student and school progress in light of standards and make changes to the curriculum and instruction as needed.

Now let us review what could be observed for several different design teams.

RW: RW accepted the Maryland state standards. We indicated such and did not expect the team to produce documents or other evidence of completion. We note, however, that the curriculum packages referred to the standards and indicated how different lessons were associated with standards. Teachers at the sites were familiar with the standards and had reviewed the design team's curriculum to ensure that it met the content and performance standards. If teachers felt that the curriculum did not meet standards they notified the team.

LALC: This team indicated that it would take existing professional standards and develop its own unique set, along with specific assessments. It was in the process of doing this at the end of Phase 2. It had developed eight broad standards and introduced these to the sites in spring 1994. However, these eight broad standards have not been translated into actual content or performance standards by grade level, which the team intends to do. Some progress has been made in this regard. We indicated that it showed beginning progress.

AT: This team said that the first job of the ATLAS Community Team (ACT) would be to develop a set of standards for the pathway and to develop exhibitions for graduation. These were to be drafted and documented by March 1994, revised soon after, and presented to the school staffs before the end of the school year in June 1994. At the time of our spring 1994 visits, sites had only initiated functioning ACTs. Neither site had developed standards or exhibitions. In the design team interview, the design team was still unclear as to what an exhibition was and what standards might be. School staff reported that they had received very unclear information from the team. By spring 1995, the ACT at each site had begun to address standards and was working on this. The requirements for graduation, exhibitions, etc., were in the process of being developed at both sites and one site had used the new graduation requirements and exhibition ideas for its first graduating class. Documentation was to be delivered by June 1995. We indicated that the design team had made moderate progress in this area.

REFERENCES

Adelman, Nancy, and Beverly Pringle, "Education Reform and the Uses of Time," *Phi Delta Kappan*, September 1995, pp. 27–29.

Berman, Paul, and Milbrey McLaughlin, *Federal Programs Supporting Educational Change, Vol. IV: The Findings in Review*, RAND, R-1589/4-HEW, Santa Monica, California, 1975.

Bimber, Bruce, *The Decentralization Mirage: Comparing Decision-making Arrangements in Four High Schools*, RAND, MR-459-GGF/LE, Santa Monica, California, 1994.

Bodilly, Susan, *Lessons from New American Schools Development Corporation's Demonstration Phase*, RAND, DRU-1176-NASDC, Santa Monica, California, 1995.

Bodilly, Susan, Susanna Purnell, Kimberly Ramsey, and Christina Smith, *Designing New American Schools, Baseline Observations on Nine Design Teams*, RAND, MR-598-NASDC, Santa Monica, California, 1995.

Cuban, Larry, "A Fundamental Puzzle of School Reform," *Phi Delta Kappan*, January 1988, pp. 341–344.

Cuban, Larry, "Reforming Again, Again, and Again," *Educational Researcher*, Vol. 19, No. 1, January 1990, pp. 3–13.

Darling-Hammond, Linda, "Policy and Professionalism," *Building a Professional Culture in Schools*, Ann Lieberman (ed.), Teachers College Press, New York, 1988, pp. 55–77.

Darling-Hammond, Linda, "Perestroika and Professionalism: The Case for Restructuring Teacher Preparation," *Excellence in Teacher Education: Helping Teachers Develop Learner-Centered Schools*, Robert McClure (ed.), National Education Association, Washington D.C., 1992, pp. 99–127.

Education Week, "From Risk to Renewal, An Education Week Special Report," February 10, 1993.

Elmore, Richard, and Milbrey McLaughlin, *Steady Work: Policy, Practice, and the Reform of American Education*, RAND, R-3574-NIE/RC, Santa Monica, California, 1988.

Firestone, W., S. Fuhrman, and M. Kirst, *The Progress of Reform: An Appraisal of State Education Initiatives*, Center for Policy Research in Education, Rutgers University, New Brunswick, New Jersey, 1989.

Fullan, Michael, *The New Meaning of Educational Change*, Teachers College Press, New York, 1991.

Gitlin, Andrew, and Frank Margonis, "The Political Aspect of Reform: Teacher Resistance as Good Sense," *American Journal of Education*, Number 103, August 1995, pp. 377–405.

Goodlad, John, *A Place Called School*, McGraw-Hill, New York, 1984.

Herman, Rebecca, and Sam Stringfield, *Ten Promising Programs for Educating Disadvantaged Students: Evidence of Impact*, Center for the Social Organization of Schools, Johns Hopkins University, Presented at the American Association Research Association Meeting, April 19, 1995.

Hill, Paul, and Josephine Bonan, *Decentralization and Accountability in Public Education*, RAND, R-4066-MCF/IET, Santa Monica, California, 1991.

Huberman, A. Michael, and Matthew Miles, "Rethinking the Quest for School Improvement; Some Findings from the DESSI Study," *Teachers College Record*, Vol. 86, No. 1, Fall 1984, pp. 34–54.

Kruse, Sharon, and Karen Seashore Louis, "Teacher Teaming-Opportunities and Dilemmas, "*Brief to Principals*, Brief No. 11, Center on Reorganization and Restructuring of Schools, University of Wisconsin-Madison, Spring 1995.

Levin, Henry, "Learning from Accelerated Schools," unpublished paper, Accelerated School Project, Stanford University, December 1993.

Liberman, Ann, et al., *Early Lessons in Restructuring Schools, National Center for Restructuring Education, Schools, and Teaching*, (NCREST), Teachers College, Columbia University, New York, August 1991.

McDonald, Joseph, "Humanizing the Shopping Mall High School," *Education Week*, April 5, 1995, p. 46.

McDonnell, Lorraine, and Norton Grubb, *Education and Training for Work: The Policy Instruments and the Institutions*, RAND, R-4026-NCRVE/UCB, Santa Monica, California, 1991.

McLaughlin, Milbrey, "The RAND Change Agent Study Revisited: Macro Perspectives and Micro Realities, "*Educational Researcher*, Vol. 19, No. 9, December 1990.

Mitchell, Karen J., *Reforming and Conforming: NASDC Principals Talk About the Impact of Accountability Systems on School Reform*, RAND, DRU-1242-NASDC, Santa Monica, California, 1995.

Muncey, D., "Individual and Schoolwide Change in Eight Coalition Schools: Findings from a Longitudinal Ethnography Study, "Paper presented at American Education Research Association Meeting, New Orleans, 1994.

Muncey, D. and P. McQuillian, "Preliminary Findings from a Five Year Study of the Coalition of Essential Schools, "*Phi Delta Kappan*, 1993, pp. 486–489.

Murphy, Joseph, and Philip Hallinger, *Restructuring Schooling, Learning from Ongoing Efforts*, Corwin Press, Newbury Park, California, 1993.

New American Schools Development Corporation, *Designs for a New Generation of American Schools: Request for Proposal*, Roslyn, Virginia, October 1991.

Policy Studies Associates, Inc., *School Reform for Youth At Risk: An Analysis of Six Change Models, Vol. I. Summary Analysis*, U.S. Department of Education, Washington, D.C., 1994.

Powell, Arthur, Eleanor Farrar, and David Cohen, *The Shopping Mall High School: Winners and Losers in the Educational Marketplace*, Houghton Mifflin Co., Boston, 1985.

Prestine, Nona, and Chuck Bowen, "Benchmarks of Change: Assessing Essential School Restructuring Efforts, "*Educational Evaluation and Policy Analysis*, Vol. 15, No. 3, Fall 1993.

Rogers, Everett, *Diffusion of Innovations*, Free Press of Glencoe, New York, 1962.

Rosenholtz, Susan, *Teacher's Workplace, the Social Organization of Schools*, Longman, New York, 1989.

Schwarz, Paul, "Needed: School-Set Standards," *Education Week*, November 23, 1994, p. 44.

Sizer, Theodore, *Horace's School, Redesigning the American High School*, Houghton Mifflin Co., New York, 1992.

Smith, Marshall, and Jennifer O'Day, "Systemic School Reform, "*Politics of Education Association Yearbook*, 1990, pp. 233–267.

Smrekar, Claire, "The Missing Link in School-Linked Services, "*Educational Evaluation and Policy Analysis*, Vol. 16, No. 4, Winter 1994.

Summers, Anita, and Amy Johnson, *A Review of the Evidence on the Effects of School-Related Management Plans*, Conference on Improving the Performance of America's Schools: Economic Choices, National Research Council, National Academy of Science, Washington D.C., October 12–13, 1994.

Turnbull, Brenda, "Using Governance and Support Systems to Advance School Improvement," *The Elementary School Journal*, Vol. 85, No. 3, 1985, pp. 337–351.

Tyack, David, "Restructuring in Historical Perspective: Tinkering Toward Utopia, "*Teachers College Record*, Vol. 92, No. 2, Winter 1990, pp. 169–191.

Usdan, Michael, "Goals 2000: Opportunities and Caveats," *Education Week*, November 23, 1994, p. 44.

U.S. Department of Labor, *SCANS, Learning a Living: A Blueprint for High Performance*, April 1992.

Williams, Walter, "Implementation Analysis and Assessment," *Policy Analysis*, Vol. 1, No. 3, Summer 1975.

Wohlstetter, Priscilla, "Getting School-Based Management Right, What Works and What Doesn't," *Phi Delta Kappan*, September 1995, pp. 22–24.